North American
Indian

North American Indian

Text by Christopher Davis
with an introduction
by Marlon Brando

Hamlyn

The Publishers wish to acknowledge the assist-
ance given them by the production team of the
Thames Television 'REPORT' documentary
'Now that the Buffalo's Gone', in particular :

Director-Producer Ross Devenish
Executive Producer Ian Martin
Research Ian Stuttard
Production Assistant Liz Neeson
Stills Sequence Tony Bulley
Editor Alan Afriat
Assistant Editor Jacqueline Ellison
Photography Mike Fash
Assistant John Welstead
Sound Sandy MacRae
Sound Assistant Ron Thomas
and the Controller of Features, Jeremy
Isaacs.

Published by
The Hamlyn Publishing Group Limited
London · New York · Sydney · Toronto
Hamlyn House, Feltham, Middlesex, England

Second Impression 1970

Printed in Great Britain by Jarrold & Sons
Limited, Norwich.

ISBN 0 600 30003 X

Contents

Int. oduction

For most people, all they know about Indians is what they see in Westerns. This book tries to tell you something nearer the truth. It tells you how white Americans treated the Indian in the past, and how they are being treated today.

I have many Indian friends, people who have devoted their lives to trying to do something for their countrymen when the rest of America would prefer to forget them. Some of them appear in this book. Indians are not just characters in films, they are people who, I believe, have been wronged and still are being wronged.

Marlon Brando

'They made us promises, more than I can remember, but they never kept but one. They promised to take our land and they took it.'

The Trail of the Indian

'It was a good winter day when all this happened. The sun was shining. But after the soldiers marched away from their dirty work, a heavy snow began to fall. The wind came up in the night. There was a big blizzard, and it grew very cold. The snow drifted deep in the crooked gulch, and it was one long grave of butchered women and children and babies, who had never done any harm and were only trying to run away.'

South Dakota, 29 December 1890. The witness, Black Elk, arrived soon after three hundred Sioux men, women and children were gunned down by the Seventh Cavalry after they had surrendered. To the white man it is known as the Battle of Wounded Knee; to the Indian as the Massacre of the Big Foot Band. It was the last battle to be fought in the United States' longest undeclared war.

The story has echoes of other conflicts in the four centuries of strife between the first Americans and their conquerors, but it remains the most emotive to the Indian of today because it was at Wounded Knee that the dream of his people was finally broken. And it was a dream. By 1890 the life that they had known and loved had already disappeared under the white invasion. The tribes had been reduced by poverty, warfare, disease, and were confined on reservations. The fighting was over, the buffalo had gone from the plains, and they were dependent for subsistence on rations

This page: **Arapaho Ghost Shirt, of the type worn by the Plains Indians for the Ghost Dance, and which the Sioux believed would protect them against the white man's bullets.**

Opposite: **the Battle of Wounded Knee ended in a blizzard and the cavalry rode away, leaving the bodies to freeze where they lay. Three days later, when the storm had subsided, the dead were uncovered. Big Foot, the Sioux leader, was among them.**

doled out by the United States government.

As so often happens with peoples faced by the empty aftermath of moral defeat, a new religion had spread through the tribes. They believed that a Messiah would come and restore to them the world they had known before the white man came. It was known as the Ghost Religion and they expressed it through a dance called the Ghost Dance. The fervour with which it swept across the Plains was indicative of the way in which the Indians had been spiritually plundered.

The Sioux, however, brought something else to their dancing. They believed that the shirts they wore for the Ghost Dance were blessed with a magic that would deflect the white man's bullets. With the bloodied garments on the field of Wounded Knee, the lie was swiftly given to this faith, and the hopes of the Indians for existing as an independent people were finally buried.

The resigned lament for the dead at Wounded Knee is typical of the way the Indian looks back on his history from the time that Columbus arrived. His hankering for a long-ago past is scarcely surprising when one considers that in 1492 there were probably more than a million Indians north of the Rio Grande, and that by the end of the nineteenth century there were not much more than two hundred thousand.

Add to this the loss of almost a whole continent in terms of land, the disruption of a culture thousands of years old, and the general myth abroad today, fostered by the legends of Hollywood and cheap 'Western' literature, that the Indian was nothing more than a marauding savage, and it is of small wonder that the majority of the half million Indians alive today are weighed down by a sense of futility and deprivation.

For the Indians, of course, their history did not begin in 1492 or in 1776, and today they remain suitably unimpressed by Columbus. 'I would say that we discovered the white man, too. At that time we hadn't known that there was land across the sea, so I think by the same

Top right: the arrival of Columbus. ' And as soon as I arrived in the Indies, in the first island that I found, I took some of them by force, to the intent that they should learn and give me information of what there was in those parts.'

Below right: an early map of the New World.

Left: the Noble Savage. An Iroquois (probably a Mohawk), drawn by Charles Bécard de Gran-ville about 1700.

Overleaf: Florida Indians of the sixteenth century. The new Queen is carried to meet the King.

token that the next time I go to England or Italy, I intend to take a flag and plant it and claim it for my Indian people, because, after all, it would be the first time that I had ever seen it, so therefore I would be discovering it.'

Not unnaturally, in 1492 they were afflicted with greater awe. 'They believed very firmly,' wrote Christopher Columbus in his first report, 'that I, with these ships and crew, came from the sky; and in such opinion they received me at every place where I landed, after they had lost their terror. And this comes not because they are ignorant; on the contrary, they are men of very subtle wit, who navigate all those seas, and who give a marvellously good account of everything...' Columbus went even further to describe them as 'artless and generous with what they have, to such a degree as no one

would believe but he who had seen it. Of anything they have, if it be asked for, they never say no, but do rather invite the person to accept it, and show as much lovingness as though they would give their hearts...'

For a man of such noble sentiments, Columbus was not exactly magnanimous in his actions. He sent 500 as slaves to Spain, and the rest were forced to work in mines and plantations. This, combined with the diseases brought by the Spaniards, meant that in less than twenty-five years the original population of Haiti of 200,000 had shrunk by three-quarters, while that of Borinquen (Puerto Rico) was reduced by 180,000 in the three years between 1508 and 1511. The Indian no longer thought Columbus came from heaven: 'We were happy when he first came. We thought that he came

from the light; but he comes like the dark of the evening now, not like the dawn of the morning. He comes like a day that has passed, and night enters our future with him.'

From then on the status of the Indian would never be the same. His privacy had been invaded, his inheritance uprooted and even the name of his country had been changed. Thereafter he would have to fit into the white man's concept of the world in order to have any assurance of survival, and it was a concept that he neither desired nor understood.

Early settlers' impressions of the Indians were varied, but the generally recorded image is one of admiring curiosity. Through those returning to Europe the concept of the Noble Savage was passed on, and eventually became part of a fashionable philosophical idea. But

quite aside from the novelty interest that their discovery had generated, the more advanced Indian tribes could hand out lessons in democracy to both the European and American continents in the sixteenth and seventeenth centuries. The Chief Kings of the East Coast tribes did not govern by any hereditary or divine right. They were elected to their positions only after they had demonstrated their fitness to rule. 'They were kings by the will of the people—not by the Grace of God.' It was this that inspired the ideal of 'government by consent of the governed', first put into words by Locke, and later incorporated, in modified form, by Jefferson in the Declaration of Independence. The irony of it is that today, when democracy is proclaimed more than ever as the watchword of American politics, the Indian

Three more drawings of Indians by Charles Bécard de Granville. They reflect the contemporary European view of the native as a guileless innocent.

benefits least of all. He is still, as it were, at the lowest end of the social pecking order.

Europe in the sixteenth and seventeenth centuries was warlike and uncharitable. It benefited the Indian not at all that he was friendly to the settlers. In the eyes of the latter it was virtually a pre-ordainment that they should subjugate the natives to their will and their code of civilization. The conquistadores were explicitly told to preach to the people they conquered that there was only one God in heaven, and one emperor on earth, whose subjects they must become. It therefore never occurred to the Spaniards that the American Indians had any right to self-determination and self-government, despite the fact that most of them had been conducting their tribal societies in just such a way for a millenium and more.

The English invaders further north were scarcely more enlightened. In 1583 Sir George Peckham wrote that 'the "savages" are to be brought from falsehood to truth, from darkness to light, from the highway of death to the path of life, from superstitious idolatry to sincere Christianity, from the devil to Christ, from hell to heaven... Beside the knowledge how to till and dress their ground, they shall be reduced from unseemly customs to honest manners, from disordered, riotous routs and companies to a well-governed commonwealth and withal shall be taught mechanical occupations, arts and liberal sciences.' Peckham's idea of making Englishmen of Americans was thought a noble sentiment, and this very approval further served to hasten the casual destruction of the native American cultures. Co-existence

Florida Indian warriors of the sixteenth century. When challenged by the Spaniards they fought tenaciously, but defeat brought vile persecution from their conquerors.

was never considered; the aggressive tendencies of the age demanded that the Indian way of life be changed, and it mattered not that forcible means were used.

Early English survival in New England was dependent on the friendship of the Indians. The Pilgrim Fathers would not have lasted their first winter had it not been for the generosity of the local natives. That generosity later gave Europe the knowledge of maize, potatoes, beans, peanuts, peppers, tomatoes, pumpkins, avocados, pineapples, tobacco, vanilla, cotton, rubber and a large number of drugs. Sadly it

was not reciprocated. The Pilgrims wer possessed of the unbending prejudice of th self-righteous. If the Indians were not Chris ians, they must be Devil-worshippers. Th feeling grew among the colonists stretche across the edge of the New World that th Indians were not only heathen but subhuma Civilization and religion could therefore b bestowed on them by the white man as a bless ing, and from this monstrous self-delusio began the encroachment on their property an on their society which continued unremitting for three centuries, and which, it can b

argued, continues even today. 'The Pilgrim Fathers fell on their knees, and then, as the saying goes, fell on the aboriginies.'

In the words of one writer, the whites became 'a horde of English tartars sweeping across the plains'. In fact it was not quite as dramatic as that. The subjugation of the Indian was achieved only step by step, and it was a complex struggle that involved destructive elements besides the conventional methods of warfare. Alcohol, disease, poverty and starvation contributed just as insidiously to their plight, not to mention the loss of their land and

the breaking of their spirit. The former was achieved largely by weapons or whisky, and by a string of broken treaties; the latter by the persistent moral blackmail that sought to convince the Indian he was an inferior being. But one consistent pattern does emerge. The Indian, when challenged, fought to the death; if he survived, he was moved westward.

Among the white settlers, the concept of the Noble Savage did not last; he was just a savage. The second great legend grew up of the perpetually murderous warrior, carrying a tomahawk in one hand and a scalp in the other.

Indians and the land from which they were driven.

'The Cherokee Mother's Last Offering', by J. G. Chapman, is a romanticized view but conveys something of the pathos attached to the removal of the Five Civilized Tribes from their rich landscape to the deserts of Oklahoma.

On the right is a late sixteenth-century drawing of an Indian community in Virginia. The English settlers who arrived there were quick to recognize the potential of an area which could produce such healthy crops of corn, tobacco and vegetables.

The Great God who is the power and wisdom that made you and me Incline your hearts to Righteousnes Love and peace. This I send to Assure you of my Love, and to desire your Love to my ffriends, and when the Great God brings me among you I Intend to order all things in such manner that we may all live in Love and peace one with another which I hope the Great God will Incline both me and you to do. I seek nothing but the hono.r of his name, and that we who are his workmanship, may do that which is well pleasing to him. The man which delivers this unto you, is my speciall ffriend Sober wise and Loving, you may believe him. I have already taken care that none of my people wrong you, by good Laws I have provided for that purpose, nor will I ever allow any of my people to sell Rumme to make your people drunk. If anything should be out of order, expect when I come, it shall be mended, and I will bring you some things of our Country that are usefull and pleasing to you. So I rest In y.e Love of our god y.t made us I am

England 2s : 2 : 1682

I writ this to the Indians by an Interpr. pr. the 6 mo 1682 Tho: Holme

your Loveing Freind

WM PENN

The pioneers were chiefly responsible for the fostering of this myth, and where it was true, they were in any case chiefly the cause of it. Many peaceful tribes became warriors because of what was done to them.

But the pioneers were an unusual breed. They were tough and greedy, and to justify to themselves the breaking of agreements and the stealing of land, psychologically they had to despise the people among whom they came. From this ill-educated band there flowed reports that the Indian was an obdurate animal who refused to acknowledge the blessings of white civilization. The feeling of contempt was further enhanced by the fact that the adventurers could not understand the Indian. They argued that he was not acquisitive, did not want gold, and resisted doing more work than was necessary to feed himself and his kin. He must therefore belong to some lowly species, undeserving of the rights of freedom or ownership. There was no alternative but to despise him. The only good Indian was a dead one.

In fairness to the whites, there were earnest efforts made by many individuals and by religious bodies to halt the persecution. But they generally floundered against the tide. A papal bull, like that of Pope Paul III in 1537, which threatened excommunication to whites who enslaved Indians, was virtually meaningless in the face of the spirit of aggression which the invaders had brought with them from a likeminded Europe. Colonial and British government measures met with a similar fate, each decree being nullified by successive events on the frontier.

As time progressed and the settlers became more 'civilized', government attempts to break the eternal warring deadlock between Indian and white man became increasingly fruitless. The liberal sentiments of a small band of intelligentsia were not sufficient to counteract the already hardened character of the new Anglo-American who was driving ever westward in pursuit of his dream of prosperity.

The Indians had to be the losers, but they were of course not wholly innocent. A number of the tribes were by nature warlike and brought the settlers' revenge down on themselves by acts of provocation and violence. Those Indians who were initially hostile had been in the habit of warring among themselves. The arrival of the colonists on their territory

offered them a chance to hunt a new prey, and the very act of settlement on their land provided them with a justification for hostilities. Others, who bore grievances against rival tribes too bitter for appeasement, sided with the English and fought their enemies that way. It was from these violent factions of the Indian nation that the overriding impression grew of a merciless and barbarous people, given to acts of outrage that repelled human dignity. By modern standards it was not untrue. Some tribes indulged in torture, human sacrifice and even cannibalism. But the same charge should be laid against the early Europeans who brought with them the last brutal vestiges of the Middle Ages, and to whom dismemberment and burning were accepted codes of punishment. In the same way that the Europeans believed such treatment to be fitting, so were the Indian practices accepted traits of the religious and social systems of the tribes that enforced them.

In fact, in the long run, it made no difference what impression the white man carried of the Indian. If it was hostile then there would be fighting, and the Indian would always have to retreat. If it was friendly, then he would be subverted by more subtle means. The well-meaning but mistaken efforts of those bodies charitable towards the Indians typify this last. By offering them the blessings of civilization and the benign blanket of Christian society, they effectively undermined the Indians' ability to deal with the hostile white men, and having robbed them of their own society and culture, discovered that they had on their hands a group of confused, disorganized peoples who simply watched helplessly as their lands were appropriated and their clansmen uprooted.

At the most callous level it could be said the colonist was only friendly to the Indians for as

Previous page and left: **William Penn's treaty with the Delawares. Penn made this treaty when he founded Pennsylvania, and it was kept faithfully for as long as he lived. When he died, however, the Delawares lost a protector, and during the next 150 years they were forced to move seven times.**

Right: **the seal of Penn's treaty.**

Far right: **in the early wars, captives on either side could seldom expect clemency.**

long as they were useful to him. Trade was an example. For a while in some areas, arrangements profitable to both sides flourished. The Indian, after all, had plenty to offer the white man in the way of valuable commodities. But it proved his undoing. A vast market for Indian goods opened up in Europe, and the white traders were swift to seize on it, capitalizing on the ignorance of the Indian to cheat him and make huge profits for themselves. Those Indians who were not providing the merchants of Europe with cumulative wealth by their forcible imprisonment in the slave trade, were finding themselves in debt to the exploiters in another sense. They became dependent on manufactured goods.

At first this made life easier for them, but gradually the inevitable moral erosion sapped their resistance and changed their way of life for the worse. When this happened and they found themselves in increasingly close contact with the white man, their defences were assaulted by the worst enemy of all – disease. The settlers brought with them diseases the Indians had never known and were powerless to resist. Over the years many more died from sickness than from warfare. Epidemics of small-pox, measles, dysentery, typhoid, tuberculosis and cholera ravaged their population, and in some cases whole tribes were wiped out. Venereal disease likewise took its toll. As if this were not enough, the white trader held in his hand one further trump card – alcohol. Here again the resistance of the Indian was pathetically low. In liquor the Indian was always useful to the white man, because through its persuasion he ceded his goods and his land. And when he had finally lost his wealth and his freedom it was to alcohol that he turned again, but this time as a means for oblivion.

The history of the American West being the history of a frontier, it is not surprising that conflicts between invader and native persistently stand out from the narrative. Measured purely in terms of time, the Indians and the whites were more often than not in friendly contact, and if one looks at a list of the major battles between 1600 and 1900, of which there were approximately seventy, almost fifty of them took place in the second half of the nineteenth century. (The latter period embraces the last stand of the fighting Indians of the Plains, and is the picture of the native most widely known today.) But while that same list will show lengthy periods of 'peace', it will also clarify better than any historical account the long retreat westward.

Major Battles with Indians (1637-1890)

Puget Sound Fights 1856
Rains Fight 1855
Four Lakes 1858
Steptoe Defeat 185[8]
Clearwater 18[ ]
Whitebird 187[ ]
Big H[ ]
Birch Creek 1878
Fette[ ]
W[ ]
Lava Beds 1873
Bear River 1863
Pyramid Lake 1860
Meeker Mas[ ]
Canyon de Chelly 1864
Big Dry Wash 1882
Salt River Canyon 1872
Apache Pass 1862

Paws 1877

Killdeer Mt. 1864

Big Mound 1863

Little Big Horn 1876
Lame Deer 1877
Whitestone Hill 1863

6
Slim Buttes 1876
56
Powder River 1876

Birch Coulee 1862

7
Dull Knife 1876
Wood Lake 1862
New Ulm 1862
Fort Ridgely 1862

Bloody Brook 1675

Swamp Fight 1675

Pequot Fort 1637

Wounded Knee 1890

865
ight 1854
Warbonnet Creek 1876

Fort Detroit
1763

Seneca Defeat 1779

Bluewater 1855
Fort Dearborn 1812
Fallen Timbers
1794
Bushy Run 1763

lk Creek 1879
Julesburg 1865
Tippecanoe 1811
St Clair Defeat 1791

Beecher's Island 1868
Point Pleasant 1774

Sand Creek 1864
Tuscarora
Defeat 1713

Adobe Walls 1864, 1874
rising 1847
Washita 1868

Palo Duro
Canyon 1874
Soldier Spring 1868
Yamasee Defeat 1715

Horseshoe Bend 1814

Fort Mims 1813
Fort Gadsden
1816
Clinch
Fight
1835
Dade
Fight 1835

Up to 1800 all the major engagements took place along the eastern seaboard, moving inland only as far as the area of the Great Lakes. A map of the lands ceded to the whites follows a parallel course, and points a stark finger at the way a whole continent was bought, lost or stolen on an ever-escalating scale as the pioneers poured westward, confining the remnants of a once great people in tiny pockets of territory from which, over wire fences, they could survey their lost inheritance and peruse their tattered history.

In the beginning of the struggle, the odds were stacked more or less equally. The Indian had knowledge of the terrain, the white man had guns. But the Indian's role was always that of the defender; no victory he won on the battleground, however complete, would remove the invader from his shores. And the invader was strengthened by what he believed to be the divine right of conquest.

The raids of the Spanish slavers along the Gulf Coast in the early sixteenth century typified this attitude. The Spaniards came searching for slaves and for wealth; the Indians fought against slavery, but lured the foreigners on in their quest for riches with tales of fabulous cities to the north. These myths led to the rival expeditions of Coronado and de Soto, both of which exemplify the barbarous treatment of the native which was standard practice for those times. De Soto landed in Florida in 1539, and set off in search of the legendary Seven Cities of Cibola. His expedition wandered for three years through the Southeast, encountering numerous Indian tribes, and leaving behind a trail of devastation and bloodshed. Villages were looted and burned, native leaders executed, and those of the tribal population that survived massacre were impressed as guides or servants. De Soto found nothing and died on the lower Mississippi, while the survivors of his band struggled back across Texas into Mexico.

Coronado, meanwhile, had pursued a similar course through Pueblo Indian country in the Southwest. The Pueblos were apparently friendly, in spite of the demands made on them in the way of food, clothing and human

Land Cessions

Key

Prior to 1784

1784 to 1810

1810 to 1850

1850 to 1870

1870 to 1890

Never formally ceded

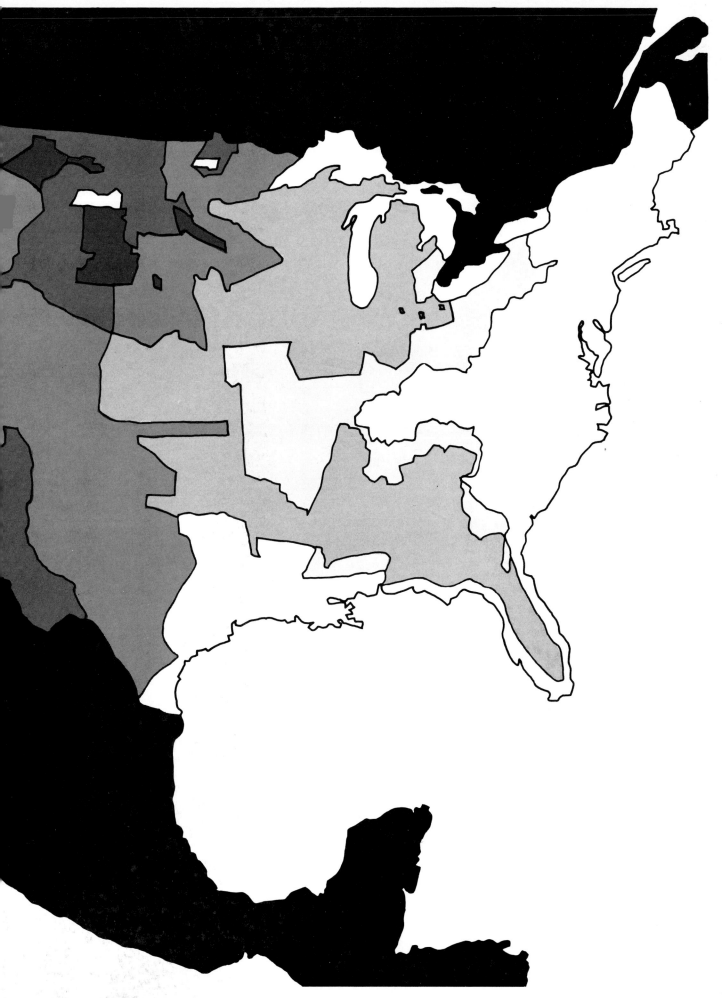

bondage, until a Spaniard raped a native woman. Then they rebelled. The uprising was squashed, and a group of several hundred surrendered after being promised pardon. Coronado, however, had other ideas. He was interested in making an example of the rebels so that the Indian population throughout the continent would learn to fear the Spaniard. Two hundred stakes were prepared. 'Then when the enemies saw the Spaniards were binding them and beginning to roast them, about a hundred men who were in the tent began to struggle and defend themselves with what there was there

achieved at enormous cost. Don Juan de Oñate's colonizing expedition in 1598, that brought soldiers and priests to New Mexico exacted its toll on the population.

Like Coronado, he sought to make an example of any insurgents. The Keres of Acoma were the first to suffer. They refused to surrender their town to be destroyed, the Spaniards attacked, killing 800 Indians and taking nearly 600 prisoners. 'The latter were tried and punished. With this the land was pacified thanks to God our Lord.' The punishments meted out included, among others, the sentenc-

The effects of the white man's invasion. The dejected group of Iroquois and the dishevelled Seneca woman with her child are typical of the plight of many of the East Coast Indians at the beginning of the nineteenth century.

and with the stakes they could seize. Our men who were on foot attacked the tent on all sides...and then the horsemen chased those who escaped. As the country was level not a man of them remained alive...'

For over two centuries this northern frontier of the Spanish Empire was a land of war, and the strength of the native resistance was such that the Spaniards were never able to consolidate their positions in what is now the United States. It is perhaps the only lasting and significant victory that the Indians ever won and explains why the Pueblo Indians of today are the most independent and self-supporting of all the native Americans. But it was a victory

ing of all males over the age of twelve to twenty years' penal servitude, and in addition all male over twenty-five were to have one foot cut off If any lenience was to be shown, it had to be done in such a way that it appeared to come a the request of the friars. In this way Oñate hoped that the Indians would look upon the friars as their benefactors and thus come to love as well as fear, their conquerors.

On the Northeast coast, as far as the India was concerned, the picture was the same. I differed only in emphasis. The French wer quick to exploit the market in furs and a patter of rivalry and bloodshed developed betwee the tribes who sought a monopoly of thi lucrative trade. The arrival of the Europeans meant the introduction of guns, powder, steel, trinkets, and other manufactured goods that appealed to the Indian and gave him prestige over his enemies. But in those early days the gun was the decisive factor. When Samuel de Champlain aided the Hurons in 1609 in their war with the Iroquois of New York, his party used muskets and incurred the bitterest resentment from the Mohawks, who had no guns and who in years to come were to revenge the injustice by siding with the British in their battles with the French.

of it was subject to the acquisitiveness rather than the altruism of the white man.

The English colonists who settled at Jamestown, Virginia, in 1607, and who believed themselves to be gentlemen adventurers, handed out the uncomfortable lesson to the Indians that, when it came to the crunch, they were more adventurers than they were gentlemen. Most of these settlers survived in the beginning by seizing or buying corn from the Indians, and aroused the resentment of Powhatan, who ruled over the strong Algonquian confederacy in the area. In one of the subse-

The Europeans were seldom to disapprove of the Indians fighting amongst themselves, nor were they slow to enlist their help, when they could get it, in their wars against other tribes or other Europeans. Thus with the steady expansion of English, Dutch, Scottish, Irish, French Huguenot, German and Scandinavian settlers along the Atlantic seaboard, the Indian was faced with a bewildering number of enemies and in time it became simply a question of expediency whose side he took. Time, however, was seldom kind to him—his allies betrayed him as they mended their own differences, and peace, if granted, was uncomfortable in its brevity because the maintaining

quent feuds, Pocahontas, Powhatan's daughter, performed her famous life-saving act over John Smith. After Pocahontas' marriage to John Rolfe, another colonist, there was peace for a time, and Powhatan came to recognize that there was benefit to be had from trading with the settlers. But by the time that he died, in 1618, the tobacco market had opened up in Europe and the whites were demanding more and more of the Indians' land to cultivate their crops.

It was the beginning of the forcible eviction which the Indian has never been able to understand. To him the land was an element, God given, no different from the sea or the air.

He had never conceived of land as being a commodity that could be traded. As Tecumseh, the great Shawnee leader, was to say two centuries later, 'a man could no more sell land than he could sell the sea or the air that he breathes...One does not sell the earth upon which the people walk'. At all events, the pressure was too great for Opechancanough, Powhatan's brother, who led an Indian attack on the colony, destroying several settlements and slaying 350 whites.

Colonial vengeance was terrible, with a war that lasted for twenty-two years and which finally smashed the Powhatan confederacy. Throughout this time the settlers carried out three punitive expeditions a year that gave the Indians no chance to plant their crops or rebuild their villages. The English captains were under orders to make no peace on any terms and to give no quarter to survivors. The standard battle strategy was to persuade the Indians to return to their villages on a promise of peace and then, when they were trapped, to massacre them. In 1625, for example, one thousand Pamunkeys were accounted for in this way, and their town destroyed. When peace eventually came in 1644, the English made separate treaties with each of the various tribes of the broken confederacy, and then assigned them to reservations which were subsequently whittled down at the colonists' pleasure. Thus, within forty years of the English arriving in Virginia the once mighty Powhatans had been reduced to confinement and beggary.

This story was repeated, with local variations, all along the Atlantic seaboard. Indians proffered friendship to the first whites they saw and lived, or died, to regret it. To the whites the slaughter or eviction of natives was purely a matter of business. While the Spaniards had gone in for a modicum of soul-searching, the English underwent no such complications of conscience. There was no official body to protect the Indians from exploitation, and the settlers were answerable to no one if they chose to indulge in enslavement or annihilation. This was later modified when the Crown took over the colonies, but by then the white had already made an enemy of the Indian.

In the early days in New England, the coastal explorers and traders were greeted with warmth and courtesy by the natives. Then one of the sea captains treacherously seized a number of them to sell in the Mediterranean slave markets. Bewildered by such high-handed treatment, the Indians reacted angrily and their

The Indians touched the pen and ceded their lands, often never knowing what it was that they signed.

Left: **a parley between white men and Pawnees at Council Bluffs, Iowa, in 1819.**

Above: **the signing of the Fort Laramie treaty in 1868 in which the Sioux were promised that they could keep the Black Hills. A few years later, when gold was found in the area, the Government condemned the Indians' title to the land.**

resentment was still smouldering when the Pilgrims nervously disembarked in 1620.

The initial survival of the new arrivals was largely due to an Indian named Squanto who had been taken to Europe as a slave and had returned. Squanto interpreted for the settlers and assisted them in making a living from the wilderness. They were also indebted to Massasoit, chief of the Wampanoag Indians, who, like Powhatan in Virginia, recognized that peaceful trading with the colonists could prove useful to his people. The era of good relations lasted until 1636, when the Massachusetts Bay Puritans, on the flimsiest of pretexts, declared war on the Pequots (a division of the Mohegans). By that time the Indians were regarded by the white clergy as agents of Satan—a brand of religious zeal that encouraged the firing of the principal Pequot town near the Mystic River in Connecticut, and the roasting to death or shooting of more than six hundred of its inhabitants. As the Plymouth governor wrote, 'It was a fearful sight to see them frying in the fire...and horrible was the stink and stench thereof. But the victory seemed a sweet sacrifice and they gave praise thereof to God...' The Pequot nation was destroyed, and the chance of peaceful co-existence in New England

had been thrown away in a fit of puritanical God-lust. It seems an almost artless footnote to add that the seal of the Massachusetts Bay Colony showed the figure of an Indian with a label at his mouth saying: 'Come over and help us'.

When Massasoit died, the Pilgrims initiated a policy of placing the Wampanoags under outright subjugation. But they had to contend with Massasoit's son, Metacom, known to the colonists as King Philip. Philip attempted to organize an alliance among the New England tribes, while at the same time seeming to bend to the colonists' demands. His attempts at forging a tribal alliance had not been completed before he was forced, under repeated provocation, to declare war. Even so, he was able to muster a sizeable force of Indians, later reinforced by the mighty Narraganset tribe, and to confront the Puritans with an army of warriors inflamed by repeated injustices. Against them were ranged the full military panoply of the English colony, inspired by the thunderings of their religious leaders.

It was the bloodiest war in New England history. The Indians had not learned sophisticated battle tactics, but they did have guns, and Philip was a gifted and resourceful leader.

Ralph Morrison, a hunter, killed and scalped by Cheyennes near Fort Dodge, Kansas, December 1868. The white man would always justify his actions against the Indian by citing instances of this practice.

Opposite above: a sixteenth-century Florida chieftain shows settlers a column, erected by an earlier French voyager, to which the natives have made offerings. From the Indians the Europeans acquired the knowledge of a variety of fruit, vegetables, raw materials and drugs.

Below: the Miami leader Little Turtle negotiating the Treaty of Greenville (1795) with Anthony Wayne. This was the first of many treaties that wrung large land cessions from the Indians, and it opened up most of Ohio and part of Indiana to the settlers.

Victory for the Puritans, however, was inevitable through sheer weight of numbers and, as before, they distinguished themselves by widespread massacres of the native population, including the noncombatant sectors, which are scarcely credible to the modern ear in either extent or method, but which must be regarded as gospel because it was the Puritans themselves who, with unmistakable relish, recorded the incidents. Philip himself was killed in the decisive battle of the war, his body quartered and the limbs distributed amongst those who had killed him. His head was displayed publicly on a pole, symbolic of the breaking of Indian power in New England. And it was broken. The individual bands of Philip's confederacy had been eliminated one by one, those who fled being hunted and slaughtered, those who stayed being shipped to the slave markets. The might of the theocracy had been threatened, but now it stood faster than ever.

The war in New England was instrumental in creating for the white man an image of the Indian that he was never to lose. From then on the settlers, as they moved westward, were to equate all Indian behaviour with the alleged savagery of Philip's war. Scalping was the most common as well as the most emotive image. True, the Indians had practised it, and would continue to do so, but it was not unknown in Europe (poachers received such treatment in England), and it was scarcely more barbarous than the punitive customs of the settlers.

In some cases, scalping was actually introduced by the whites to tribes who had never practised it. To the pioneers, however, it would always remain an affront to human dignity, and as they moved across the face of the continent they carried with them the thought that if they fell into Indian hands, they would undoubtedly be scalped. This led them to commit innumerable acts of unsolicited violence against the natives, which inevitably brought retaliation and of course the payment in kind which they had specifically feared. Thus the image of the Indian became an increasingly savage one, and it was a vicious circle from which he was never given enough time or peace to break.

Rivalry between European powers over land and Indian furs meant continual skirmishing, either between European and Indian, or between the Indians themselves. Tribes either disappeared or were displaced. In the east, only the powerful Iroquois achieved a measure of independence, which they managed through a mixture of skilful diplomacy and calculated aggression.

The League of the Six Nations of the Iroquois held sway both over the lesser tribes in the region and over the settlers' internecine wranglings. By declaring themselves impartial, the Iroquois were in a strong bargaining position with both the French and the English, for each side was anxious to add them to their military strength. When the Seven Years War broke out, the Iroquois took up an officially neutral stand, but in fact they gave both direct and indirect aid to the British. Their geographical position across the St Lawrence and their control of the principal routes that connected eastern Canada with the French positions in the Ohio Valley and Louisiana hampered the French considerably, and when

Above and below left: two views of the Trail of Tears. Pushed along by the soldiers, the tribes suffered untold hardship. Four thousand Cherokees, nearly a quarter of their nation, died of starvation and disease.

Right: Thomas Jefferson, who for all his liberalism initiated the 'harsh' policy that led to the Indian Removals.

the war was over, and the British were dominant in North America, the Iroquois were rewarded with the promise of respectful treatment by the victors.

That was fine for the Iroquois but not so good for the lesser tribes, for whom the Iroquois had previously spoken in council, and who had sided with the French. They were faced by an arch Indian-hater in General Jeffery Amherst, commander of the British and colonial forces. Amherst issued strict regulations that banned the credit and gifts which these Indian tribes had been accustomed to receiving from the French. As a result the inland tribes, confronted also by the renewed westward migration of white settlers, retaliated by grouping themselves under Pontiac and attacking every British-held post, including Detroit, which Pontiac besieged for five months. As with the earlier wars, the Indians were successful for a time, and then their resistance was broken. With no real prospect of a lasting victory, the tribal unity could not be maintained. Pontiac, faced by defection and the hopelessness of his cause, surrendered. Those who had taken part in the war—Delawares, Shawnees, Ojibwas, Potawatomis, Miamis, Weas, Senecas, Kickapoos—were once more adrift and dependent on white clemency. It came in an unpalatable form. Army officers introduced smallpox among the tribes, with savage success. It was another British victory.

With the outbreak of the American Revolution, the colonists had to perform a complete *volte-face* in their dealings with the Indians. To prevent the tribes from siding with the British, they issued orders that stopped the trespassing on Indian lands. In some places settlers were turned back and the tribes further mollified with gifts of gunpowder for their hunting. But it was not enough. When hostilities began in the Northeast the Iroquois divided, some siding with the colonists, and a large force under Thayendanegea, a Mohawk chief better known as Joseph Brant, joined the British. Brant became a feared warrior, allegedly responsible for savage raids and massacres

which earned him a reputation he did not really seek, for he was gifted with statesmanlike qualities that could have greatly benefited his people in times of peace. When the war ended he crossed with his division of the Iroquois into Canada, and the power of the Six Nations was split in two. They continue in close association even today, but from the end of the American Revolution their strength as a unified buttress against the encroachments of the white man was sharply diminished.

Under the new American government the Indians fared little better than they had done under British rule. No law passed, however well-meaning, could counteract the unscrupulous dealings of the traders and settlers along the frontiers. Government control was powerless against the pressure of the private trading companies. The Indian was driven back, and he retaliated. Wars broke out in the Northwest, the Indians won a couple of victories before suffering the inevitable crushing defeat, and treaties followed that ceded most of Ohio, a part of Indiana and strategic areas of the so-called Northwest Territory. The ceded lands filled up with the tide of white settlers, peace lasted for a while, the settlers grew greedy and started to push further west, the Indian complained, and the circus began all over again. War, defeat, treaty, land yielded. No matter how many castles the Indian built they were all made of sand. No matter, either, if he chose to be friendly or hostile. His land would fall to the white men, and the white men knew they would get it. It was now God's own country and therefore, by tortuous logic, theirs. Any means of bribery would do. Even Benjamin Franklin was to declare that rum should be used to 'extirpate these savages in order to make room for the cultivators of the earth'.

During the first decade of the nineteenth century, when it seemed to the Indians that there was little hope of preventing the pale-faces from taking over the continent, the most visionary of their leaders appeared. Tecumseh was a Shawnee war chief, and his dream was of an Indian confederacy that would produce a

Tecumseh, one of the greatest of Indian leaders, whose vision of a separate Indian nation raised the hopes of his peoples but came too late to stem the tide.

Overleaf: **the Indians lost their lands and moved on, condemned to impermanence.**

This page: Osceola, chief
of the Seminoles, who led
his tribe in a furious war
that saved them from
wholesale eviction to the
Indian Territory.

Opposite: the Creek war of
1813–14, in which Andrew
Jackson first came
into national prominence
with his massive victory
at Horseshoe Bend.

separate nation and which would be respected by the white man. He sought to establish a firm border between the two peoples. Tirelessly he travelled the length of the country, from Florida to the Great Lakes, in an effort to unite the tribes, urging them to work together so that the land could be held in common as an inheritance for their children. It was he who first thundered against the whole concept of buying and selling land – 'Sell a country! Why not sell the air, the clouds and the great sea...?'

He was aided in his campaign by his brother Tenskwatawa, known as the Shawnee Prophet, who preached against intermarriage with the white man, the wearing of his clothing, the drinking of his liquor, and the other debilitating influences on the Indian way of life which the settlers had brought with them. The oratory and passion with which the two Shawnee brothers worked among the tribes sparked off a fervent revival of the Indian spirit, but it was not total and it came too late. Many of the older Indian chiefs were too dispirited by the events of the preceding years to be roused from their listless resignation, and the Indian frontier continued to be eroded by the land-grabbers.

Tecumseh was eventually forced into war by the high-handed methods of William Henry Harrison, the territorial governor of Indiana, who was set on evicting all Indians from the Northwest Territory. Unfortunately for the Indian cause, Harrison chose to attack Tecumseh's headquarters on the Tippecanoe River when the leader was away. Tenskwatawa, in the

absence of his brother, decided upon an ill-conceived battle plan, was driven back, his village burned and his powers as a prophet discredited.

From then on Tecumseh's hopes of a pan-Indian union had no chance of becoming reality. But he did not give up. The next year, 1812, when war again erupted between the British and the Americans, he joined the British, and his military ability played a substantial part in their early successes. He believed that if they could conquer the Americans there would be some hope of achieving his dream, and it is possible that had he been able to persuade the Iroquois to ally themselves to the British in battle, a military victory at least might have been won. But they were defeated, and Tecumseh was slain in the battle on the Thames River in 1813.

As a leader and as a statesman Tecumseh was respected by both sides, for not only was he skilful in diplomacy, he also showed humane qualities in war which the whites were not accustomed to believing an Indian could possess. Tecumseh spared those he made captive and never resorted to pointless slaughter of non-combatants, and he urged that all Indians should practise such methods in warfare and thus win the respect of the Americans. The tragedy of his vision of the Indian nation lay both in its brilliance and its timing. Perhaps half a century earlier it *could* have worked, though even that may be flattering the magnanimity of the white man and the resolution of the Indian. But by the time of Tecumseh,

The Second Seminole War lasted for seven years and cost the Americans more than two thousand dead and more than forty million dollars.

American policy towards the natives had hardened. It was, quite simply, to clear them out, and those that had not moved on with their tribes to take up defensive positions further west, were now lingering east of the Ohio in scattered bands, dejected remnants who had lost their lands and their will to live. If the fighting Indian represented a savage to the white man, the defeated Indian was a creature of pitiful squalor, and therefore even more of a burden.

The US government, confirmed in its policy of driving all Indians west of the Mississippi, had now to deal with the four great nations of the Southeast—the Creeks, Chicasaws, Choctaws and Cherokees. These peoples, together with the Seminoles, breakaways from the Creeks, later came to be known as the Five Civilized Tribes because they had, in the main, prospered under the colonial invasion. They recognized early on that the white man was there to stay and that they might as well make the most of it. Accordingly, they had acquired livestock, learned farming methods, and even in some cases adopted European clothing and housing. They had managed to conduct their trading with the settlers in a more mutually beneficial way than the tribes of the north, and intermarriage with the whites had served to increase their overall prosperity.

Not that the conversion was placid. The eighteenth century in the Southeast was a tangle of inter-tribal and inter-European struggles. The Choctaws, hereditary enemies of the Chicasaws, sided with the French; the Chicasaws, perhaps the greatest warriors of

them all, allied themselves to the British, together with the Creeks, while the Cherokees, inscrutable mountain people, preferred to stay clear of the white man's squabbles. Inevitably land cessions were wrung from them which created tension, but by the end of the century there was still a strong feeling among these tribes that it was better to react peacefully to the invader, to learn his arts and become accepted by him as a civilized equal.

The American Revolution, and the subsequent US policy, had the effect of inducing tribal schizophrenia and dividing the Indians of the Southeast against themselves. On the one side, there were those, particularly among the Creeks and the Cherokees, who were making great efforts to prove themselves peaceful, progressive people. Missionaries were invited to help and open schools; churches and roads were built. The search for self-improvement was given further impetus by the labours of Sequoyah, a Cherokee who, though not educated himself, devised a Cherokee alphabet.

Previously the missionaries had only taught in English, because they thought the Indian language could not be written. Progress was therefore slow and enthusiasm blunted. But when, after twelve years' work, Sequoyah had mastered his system for writing the Cherokee language, everyone in his tribe wanted to learn and within months thousands could read and write. The Cherokees printed a newspaper and the Creeks produced a Bible. Laws were put into writing, and the Indians were proving that in a relatively short period of time they could, on their own initiative, catch up with the

The Indians held out in the swampy Everglades of Florida in villages such as the one depicted above.

Europeans. In fact they were too successful. 'We were so civilized we had black slaves,' a tribal leader has said. By the 1820s and 1830s the Cherokees had established the first public school system in the South and had adopted a system of government modelled on that of the United States. But they were no longer a united tribe. More than six thousand, a quarter of the tribe, had disassociated themselves from these radical developments and, wishing to preserve their Indianness, had migrated as a group west of the Mississippi.

The Creeks suffered a more serious division. They had been bludgeoned by the land-speculators into ceding large parts of their territory in Georgia, with the result that many had gone to join Tecumseh to resist the white advances. The tribe split into factions, and civil war followed. The anti-American faction, known as the Red Sticks, overran Fort Mims and massacred 350 settlers. Reprisal followed under the leadership of Andrew Jackson who, with the aid of the pro-white Creeks, destroyed the Red Stick forces at Horseshoe Bend (1814). Three hundred women and children were taken prisoner, and of the 900 Red Stick soldiers only seventy survived.

With the usual tragic irony the White Sticks who had assisted the Americans in this victory were forced to sign a treaty in the same year that ceded almost two-thirds of the Creek nation's territory. The military victory, however, brought Jackson wide recognition, and his fame increased to national adulation when he invaded Spanish-held Florida in pursuit of the remaining anti-American Creeks who had fled

to live with the Seminoles. The subsequent war dispersed the Indians and ended with Spain ceding Florida to the United States. It was the finish of Spanish rule in the Southeast and therefore a blow to the Indians, for they were no longer useful to the Americans as buffer states against foreign menace. The Seminoles were persuaded into a reservation, and Andrew Jackson was elected President of the United States as the living embodiment of the frontier spirit, a man dedicated to the policy of Indian eviction. It signalled the beginning of possibly the darkest chapter in American history.

The Indian Removal Bill, which Jackson pushed through Congress in 1830, was the culmination of a rising governmental prejudice against the Indian. Its seeds were apparent even under the regime of the reputedly liberal Jefferson at the turn of the century. Jefferson may not have been specifically anti-Indian in the same sense as were many of his contemporaries, but he displayed a readiness to adopt the expedient measure where they were concerned rather than the philanthropic one. His writings betray him. In 1806 he wrote to a European: 'It may be regarded as certain that not a foot of land will ever be taken from the Indians without their own consent. The sacredness of their rights is felt by all thinking persons in America as much as in Europe'. Six years later he was to announce that 'we shall be obliged to drive them with the beasts of the forest into the stony mountains'. Jefferson's ideal of racial assimilation through intermarriage had fallen under the unyielding hammer of the frontiersmen, and he had ordered

45

his lieutenants to begin the systematic appropriation of all Indian lands east of the Mississippi. By 1809 more than 100 million acres had been acquired by one method or another. The Upper Cherokees volunteered to become citizens of the United States so that they could own their lands in severalty, but Jefferson decreed that they should move west with the others. There was now to be no retreat from the 'harsh' policy, and the Indian Removal Bill had the crushing emphasis of inevitability.

Jackson pretended to see the Bill as a remedy that would release the natives from their tribulations. And it was true that they were being tormented by the white trash. In spite of all the earlier treaties and guarantees designed to protect the Indian in his property, the squatters, speculators, traders and bootleggers had moved in and were plying their sordid business. The Southern planters needed more land, and the Indians were astride the lush mountain passes of Carolina and Georgia that led west. Alcohol was the means of persuasion, and the natives had already shown that they

were ungovernably susceptible to it. A sense of panic grew in them as their communities were infiltrated by the hungry whites, and they tended to go on drunks that lasted for days and which ended either in death or in their impressed removal.

Jackson's government wearied of the endless Indian appeals and decided they were powerless to help them. The Bill decreed nothing more than the exchange of lands in the west for those they already occupied, and was therefore dressed up as a humanitarian measure. But the Indian nations did not want to move. Jackson therefore decided that force was necessary, and his determination to evict the natives was further hardened when gold was discovered in the mountains. Into the wilderness of Oklahoma the tribes were driven along the Trail of Tears. It was an exodus of exceptional hardship and misery. Some went resignedly, some in chains, and the troops were always on hand to keep them moving. Thousands died on the march, and the wretched knots of refugees who struggled into Oklahoma were

unrecognizable as the once proud members of the great Indian confederacies of the South.

The Choctaw removal, which began in November 1831 and lasted for three successive winters, was particularly brutal. In the face of opposition from their people, the Choctaw chiefs had signed a treaty allowing it. It was an extremely severe winter. There was heavy snow in the great Arkansas swamp through which the emigrants had to pass, and because they had left their homes destitute many were barefoot and nearly naked. Money had been allocated by Congress to pay the expenses of the emigration, but much of it never reached its destination. It was disbursed through white agents and contractors who had agreed to 'conduct' the natives to their new territories for a fee. They expected to make a profit, but worse, they scarcely fulfilled their mission. Major Armstrong, for example, who was the appointed Choctaw agent for the winter of 1831 and who had been provided with $50,000 in cash to meet the expenses of the removal, decided that the weather was too inclement for him to leave his home town of Nashville, Tennessee, and accordingly did not appear with the funds until the end of February. By then it was too late.

In 1836 the entire Creek nation was forcibly marched west, and the Chicasaws followed the year after. The Cherokees resisted with extraordinary tenacity, and under their leader, John Ross, succeeded in taking their case to the United States Supreme Court. They imagined they had won a great victory when Chief Justice John Marshall, in a passionate denunciation of the Indian persecution in Georgia, persuaded the Supreme Court to uphold the Indian case and sustain their right to their Southeastern territories. But President Jackson refused to execute the decision, and the army was ordered to evict the tribe. As they prepared to go, the Georgia whites gleefully harassed and plundered them, and when they did depart, they suffered worst of all. Four thousand, nearly a quarter of the Cherokee nation, died on the march of disease and starvation. While this emigration was in progress Jackson felt able to

The homes of the nomads.

Left: **'Blackfoot Indian Encampment. Foothills of the Rocky Mountains', painted by William Armstrong.**

Right: **Sioux tipis captured after the 1862 uprising.**

Overleaf: **'Funeral Scaffold of a Sioux Chief', by Carl Bodmer.**

say that the government's handling of the Indian problem had been 'just and friendly throughout; its efforts for civilization constant ...directed by the best feelings of humanity'.

In the summer of 1831 an epidemic of cholera broke out, and a fresh one followed each summer until 1836. It set up 'a belt of death that halted most traffic, but through which the armies of Indian exiles had to be moved, the federal government and the states concerned being inflexibly opposed to any delays'. In the way of desperate people, trapped by disease

and pursued by hostile pressures, the Indian often quarrelled among themselves. They coul envisage no future and they had been severed from their past to which they were attache by the great tribal bonds of birthplace and heritage. They had left behind them their land which was sweet and luxuriant, and for which they felt an affection the settlers never under stood. There are stories of Indians, on the point of departure from their homes, wander ing about touching leaves, trees, rocks and streams in the most tactile gestures of farewel

Left: a Choctaw village. The women work while the men drink. In the Southeast the tribes were harassed by bootleggers who knew only too well their susceptibility to alcohol.

Right: the Indians of the Plains lived by a culture that was built around two animals—the buffalo and the horse. With the extinction of the buffalo their lives were starved of excitement.

while whites looked on, some in emotion, others in amusement. The Indians could not comprehend the reason for their removal and could find no justification for the oppressive visitations of their journey. 'We were drove off like wolves... and our peoples' feet were bleeding with long marches. We are men...we have women and children, and why should we come like wild horses?'

Alexis de Tocqueville, in his book *Democracy in America*, has recorded the melancholy spectacle of the removals: 'No cry, no sob was heard among the assembled crowd; all was silent. Their calamities were of ancient date and they knew them to be irremediable'. He discerned how the Indians were sent westwards by government agents: 'half convinced and half compelled they go to inhabit new deserts, where the importunate whites will not let them remain ten years in peace. In this manner do the Americans obtain at very low price whole provinces which the richest sovereigns of Europe could not purchase.'

When an attempt was made to coerce the

Seminoles of Florida into the general removal, they decided to fight it out. Under the fiery leadership of Osceola they engaged in a war that lasted for seven years, and which was enormously costly to the Americans both in terms of dollars and lives lost. The determination of the Seminoles was exemplified by the women who, like some of the Creek women earlier, killed their children in order to be free to fight beside their men. Osceola himself was treacherously seized by the Americans during a parley under a white flag, and died in prison in 1838. But the resistance of his tribe was such that they prolonged the fight in the Florida Everglades until 1842, when a peace was agreed. Many of the tribe were shipped west to the Indian Territory, but several thousand held out in the swamps, defying all subsequent blandishments to emigrate and remaining more or less at war with the whites until quite recently. On a broad front, however, the government had been ruthlessly successful in driving the Indians from the lands it coveted, and in justifying the plight of the native by the

cumulative wealth it had acquired for the country in the process.

Jackson's promise to the emigrant tribes was that their new territorial grants would endure 'as long as the grass grows, or water runs'. The hollow echoes of that phrase still ring in the Indian mind. They should never have taken note of it for, even as they were emigrating, the first fingers of the white invasion were already clutching at the lands across the Mississippi and what happened west of that river was a repeat of the chapter of events in the east—warfare, broken treaties, expropriation of land, rebellion and, ultimately, defeat. No sooner were the emigrant Indians dumped in the west than natural resources were discovered there. White settlers, miners and traders advanced along trails and railroads, and once more the Indian was an unwitting obstacle to 'progress'. The Eastern Indians had also to contend with their counterparts who inhabited the lands into which they were driven and who were not surprisingly aggrieved at this enforced occupation of their territory. The government

The Sun Dance, in which
the Plains Indians inflicted
extraordinary tortures
upon themselves to
heighten their visions and
prove their devotion. The
Sun Dance can still be seen
today.

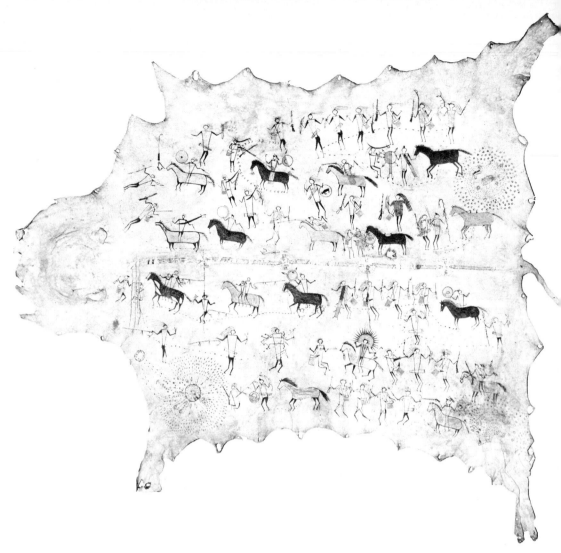

The buffalo provided the
Indians with their food,
their clothing and their
shelter. The hides were
also put to decorative use,
painted with figures of
historical or mythological
significance.

The Indians were reduced to a rabble, dependent on the white man's goods for their survival.

seeking to ease its conscience over the removals, made half-hearted attempts to keep the peace, but they were of little practical value and thus, as before, it became Indian against Indian for the benefit of the whites.

Where the Indian is concerned, the history of the nineteenth century in the West is a catalogue of bitterness. For all the glamour of defiance, and the many fighting heroes of his peoples, the reality is a shabby despair, marked by the broken pledges, fraudulent treaties and callous logic of the white men who came and offered but two alternatives—confinement or extermination. In spite of this the Indian persisted in treating the white man as his equal, in taking him at his word and trusting in the promises of the Great White Father in Washington, and yet, up to 1868, almost 400 treaties had been made and duly broken. Too late he realized that these treaties had been nothing more than instruments to prise him from his territory, real estate deals designed to take way the best land and leave him with the worst. It was the poorest land, often totally unusable, that became the reservations in which he was finally penned. He had no space to move or think. The tent of his dreams had been carried away by the gale of avarice that had swept the continent, he had lost his spirit, and his beliefs had no currency in the New World.

The rebellions of the fighting tribes in the 1870s and 1880s were in fact the last frenetic spasms of a people who were already defeated. By then the Indian had been psychologically overthrown, his efforts at co-existence nullified by the broken agreements, and his hopes for the retention of his independent way of life withered by the restrictive measures of his conquerors. In effect he was an outlaw, for in 1871 Congress ended further treaty-making with the tribes by a law decreeing that henceforth 'no Indian nation or tribe within...the United States shall be acknowledged or recognized as an independent nation, tribe or power'. Many tribes had already moved resignedly into reservations; others refused to tolerate the persistent provocations of the United States military, and reckoned it better to die than submit. Defeat was inevitable, but war at least brought a quickening of the spirit and a means of forgetting. It was in fact the Indians' last stand.

Earlier, the ravages on their land and population had been as systematically predictable as the hardening of white opinion against them. A Kansas newspaper of the 1850s summarized white feelings of the time: 'A set of miserable, dirty, lousy, blanketed, thieving, lying, sneaking, murdering, graceless, faithless, gut-eating skunks as the Lord ever permitted to infect the earth, and whose immediate extermination all men, except Indian agents and traders, should pray for'. The summoning of higher powers was superfluous: the white man's disease was doing its work, moving ahead of the advancing settlers and weakening the Indians' resistance before they were forced to negotiate or fight. Smallpox reduced the powerful Mandan tribe to a handful, and did the same by the Hidatsa. The Blackfoot population was halved, while the Kiowa and Comanche were decimated by cholera. It has been recorded that smallpox was deliberately introduced on occasions by the despatch of infected blankets from the hospitals to the reservations. Once the disease had a hold there was no means of preventing an epidemic.

Push, push, push. The settlers came from the east, crowding the Indian out, coveting his land and scorning his Indianness. The latter could be broken by the implanting of civilization, by intermarriage and manufactured goods, by guns, whisky, and venereal disease. The white traders and trappers attracted the Plains Indians, but induced inter-tribal warfare. The Plateau Indians felt the beckoning of

Christianity, but lost their tribal stability. Wars developed from skirmishes that developed from panics. The panics developed from the various nettles of the white invasion – trespass, disease, hypocrisy. In the Northwest, for example, an era of wars was begun when Cayuses panicked under the stress of an epidemic of measles and murdered the Whitmans, who ran the mission of Waiilatpu. But they were also suffering, as were other tribes in the area, from apprehension as the trickle of settlers along the Oregon Trail had grown to a flood, and their lands were threatened.

The newcomers showed scant respect. In southwestern Oregon, Rogue River Indian. clashed with miners who had treated them contemptuously. In Washington Territory the governor, I.I.Stevens, harried the tribes into ceding large portions of territory so that a rail road could be built from Minnesota to Puge Sound. Resentment flared into violence, the tribes were defeated in war, and their lands lef free for the settlers. By 1858 the Yakimas Cayuses, Wallawallas, Spokanes, Palouses and Coeur d'Alenes had been subjugated and herded onto reservations.

These pages and previous page: **the pioneers came first, and the soldiers followed after, making the Trails safe for the wagon trains. The greed of the prospectors allowed them no latitude in their dealings with the native. As a direct result of the 1849 gold rush, tens of thousands of Indians perished in California.**

Along the other great trail, to Santa Fe, Americans incurred the hostility of the Comanches and the Yuman tribes. Trappers in Nevada and Utah shot defenceless Gosiute and Paiute Indians for sport. In Texas, which had filled up with the same Indian-haters who had driven them from the southeast, the Karankawas were virtually wiped out. The natives of California suffered the most vicious persecution of all. Their villages and hunting grounds were inundated and obliterated by the gold rush, and such was the ruffian nature of the adventurers no quarter was given to the incumbents. Indians were reckoned as vermin, the men thrown into slavery, the women into prostitution. Disease followed with its scythe, and it is estimated that in the decade between 1849 and 1859 as many as seventy thousand Indians perished from one cause or another in California. In the midst of all this the occasional wry joke gave brief respite to the native in his tribulations. The Osage, for instance, were forced at gunpoint from their lush pastures onto a stretch of arid territory. It was later discovered that this land concealed one of the richest oil deposits in North America.

In the 1850s the buffalo-hunting tribes still roamed the Great Plains. They were a remarkable people and their decline from the kingship of the prairies to the pauperism of the reservations is one of the epic falls of history, remaining for all the romantic bravura of their defiance a tale of abject sadness. Beneath the Big Sky they had built a culture that fed their nomadic spirit and gave point to the visions they constructed about themselves.

Their culture was built around two animals. The first was the buffalo. At the beginning of the nineteenth century enormous herds spread across the vast expanses of the midwest, perhaps as many as sixty million. These the Indian hunted. They provided him with his chief source of food, his clothing and his shelter, and they sublimated his existence. The second animal was the horse, which had been reintroduced to America by the Spanish and which had revolutionized the Indian's life. It made his hunting easier and his warring more lethal. It broke the bonds that tied him to the earth and pampered his temptations to dream. As a result the Plains Indians became the most mystical of all Indian peoples. In a country where they could ride for ever they became fanatically proud and fanatically religious, inflicting extraordinary self-tortures on themselves to prove their devotion and to create visions that would override the pain.

The state of enchantment did not last. The emigrant wagon trains drove the buffalo from the hunting grounds, and the Plains Indians suffered the same despotic treatment as was handed out all over the West. It seemed that the tension might be eased when government agents induced the tribes to gather at Horse Creek, Wyoming, in 1851, to sign a general

peace that defined the hunting grounds and promised unmolested passage to the whites along the Trail. It was the greatest assembly of Indians in the history of the plains, with perhaps 10,000 tribespeople present, representing the Assiniboins, Atsinas, Arikaras, Crows, Shoshonis, Sioux, Cheyennes, and Arapahos, many of whom had never met before except on the battlefield.

Three years later this great peace council was rendered meaningless by an absurd incident involving the slaughter of an apparently emigrant cow by a Minneconjou Sioux. The white owner claimed recompense, which was not forthcoming in sufficient quantity, and a fire-eating lieutenant led a troop of soldiers in an impulsive punitive attack on the Sioux. The wars in the Plains had opened, and they were based, as were the other conflicts, not on the straightforward principles of revenge, but on the subversive pressure for property. As General George Crook, the most widely experienced of the Indian-fighters, was to say: 'Greed and avarice on the part of the whites – in other words, the almighty dollar, is at the bottom of nine-tenths of all our Indian troubles'.

When the Civil War broke out it was white man against white man, and the hopes of the Indian revived. For once the attack was not directed at him; and the hostilities elsewhere had slowed the westward migration of settlers.

It was, however, a false dawn. Trouble flared again in eastern Colorado where the Cheyennes and Arapahos were forced to sign a treaty that would permit the building of a railroad through what remained of their territory. There were minor skirmishes with troops but the two Cheyenne leaders, Black Kettle and White

Antelope, quickly concluded an armistice, believing as they did that peaceful negotiation was the only hope for their people. The US military remained distrustful, thinking that the leeway which the Civil War had allowed the Indians was potentially dangerous. As a result the Cheyenne suffered two of the most savage massacres in the history of the West, which were the more brutal for being unprovoked. Colonel J. M. Chivington led the first, on 29 November 1864, when the Cheyennes were encamped at Sand Creek. Three hundred men, women and children were slaughtered in the surprise attack, and the troops returned jubilant to Denver with the scalps, including that of White Antelope.

'The command of Colonel Chivington was composed of about one thousand men; the village of the Indians consisted of from one hundred to one hundred and thirty lodges, and, as far as I am able to judge, of from five hundred to six hundred souls, the majority of which were women and children; in going over the battleground the next day I did not see a body of man, woman, or child but was scalped, and in many instances their bodies were mutilated in the most horrible manner – men, women, and children's privates cut out, etc.'

As a result of Chivington's barbarity the conflagration of war spread across the plains, and with the Civil War now ended, the army redirected its attack on the tribes. Black Kettle, committed to passive resistance, made persistent efforts to restore peace for the Cheyennes, which appeared to have been successful when they were subjected to a second surprise raid. The tribe were camped on the Washita River in the autumn of 1868. The US Cavalry attacked

Previous page: the Indian spoke with eloquence to plead for peace, time, and the freedom to hunt.

Left: **Sitting Bull. He was killed by Red Tomahawk, an Indian policeman (photographed, *right*, on Sitting Bull's horse), when the cavalry, nervous at the degree to which the Ghost Dance was sweeping the plains, attempted to arrest the Sioux chief. Sitting Bull refused to surrender his arms and was shot dead.**

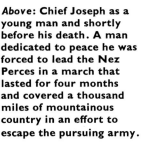

Above: **Chief Joseph as a young man and shortly before his death. A man dedicated to peace he was forced to lead the Nez Perces in a march that lasted for four months and covered a thousand miles of mountainous country in an effort to escape the pursuing army.**

at dawn, slaying one hundred and fifty, including Black Kettle. The architect of this 'victory' was Lieutenant-Colonel George Custer.

The Oglala Sioux, under Red Cloud, won a notable triumph when they refused to negotiate a settlement that would permit a passage along the Powder River to the gold fields of Montana. The government constructed forts and the Sioux besieged them, eventually forcing them to be abandoned. Red Cloud subsequently signed a peace treaty in 1868, in which he vowed never to make war again on the white man and in which the government reserved the Black Hills in perpetuity for the Sioux. Red Cloud kept his word, the government did not. Gold was discovered in the mountains, and the Sioux had to be persuaded from them. The Black Hills being sacred to them, the Sioux declined to be moved, and the government, virtually condemning their title to the land, ordered them onto reservations. The failure of the tribes to report at the agencies by the appointed date led to the order sent to General Crook to begin the final round-up.

It is scarcely surprising that the Indians refused to submit to a policy of eviction and confinement. They saw what was slipping away from them, and they heard that the future held no promise of fulfilment. On the Plains the great buffalo herds were being decimated, sometimes casually, sometimes as part of a deliberate policy to starve the tribes and force

them into captivity. As for the reservations they were in many cases run by fanatica missionaries, over-zealous in their duties an constantly split by inter-denominationa schisms, while the agencies were imbued wit corruption. President Grant's Peace Policy aimed at reforming the running of the India enclosures, was sterile in practice and a lie i name, allowing the Indians no show of inde pendence once they had submitted, and ir directly encouraging those still free to fight fo their self-esteem. In any case the tribes sti roaming across the unceded country were b now branded as bandits. There was no choice

The last and most dramatic of the Plains war began when the Cheyennes were attacked b Crook's cavalry in March 1876. An inconclusiv skirmish followed, and both sides retired t regroup. The Cheyennes allied themselve with the Oglala Sioux under Crazy Horse, an the Hunkpapa Sioux, under Sitting Bul (Red Cloud, true to his word, remained apar from hostilities.) The military, more fiercel determined than ever to whip these tribe launched a three-pronged assault. Crazy Hors engaged the southern prong, under Crook, a Rosebud Creek in southern Montana and halte the advance, retiring afterwards to link up wit the large division of Sioux and Cheyenne force camped on the Little Big Horn River. Furthe north, the two other prongs of the army ha met and decided to move south, hoping to tra

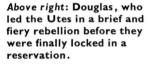

Above right: Douglas, who led the Utes in a brief and fiery rebellion before they were finally locked in a reservation.

Above left: Geronimo, who held out with his band of Chiricahua Apaches in the rocky country of the Southwest. Their final surrender excited great interest and they were photographed (*overleaf*) wherever they went. The Indian already belonged to the American legend.

the Indians between themselves and Crook's company. Ignorant of the latter's repulse, a regiment of the elite Seventh Cavalry under Custer advanced ahead of the main columns to scout. Learning of the Indian encampment, Custer rashly decided to attack with the well-known result. Two hundred and twenty-five cavalry dead, the remainder scrambling to escape, in a battle that lasted less than half an hour. Custer paid with his life, and it was a sweet revenge for the Indians after his barbarity on the Washita River.

It is important from the point of view of the Indian to put this battle in perspective. In the same way that Wounded Knee later became, in white parlance, the 'victory' at Wounded Knee, so did Little Big Horn become a 'massacre', as though the Indians were in some way the culprits. It is part of the myth that still works against them. Certainly it was a massacre, but Custer bought it, choosing as he did to attack an enemy force several times the size of his own.

Custer had become a dedicated Indian-hater after the Civil War, when he saw an opportunity to gain prestige in white political circles by winning golden opinions in the campaign against the Indians. He was a showman and a bully, riding into battle with trumpets blaring, punishing his troops when victory was not forthcoming. The defeat at Little Big Horn was the result of his vaulting ambition and his

military folly, but it was turned into a national catastrophe by its unexpectedness and its timing. The eastern seaboard knew nothing until they opened their newspapers on the morning of 5 July 1876, the day after they had been celebrating the centenary of the Declaration of Independence. For the white sophisticates it was more than a defeat, it was an indignity. The savages must be harried to the point of submission.

And they were. In this sense the Indian victory at Little Big Horn was the beginning of the last defeat. Crazy Horse and his Oglala were eventually forced by hunger to surrender in May 1877. The next year, the northern Cheyennes, exiled to malarial country in Oklahoma, escaped and, under Dull Knife and Little Wolf, made an epic march in an attempt to reach their former hunting grounds in Montana, but the hardships of the trek and the repeated attacks of the troops finally overwhelmed them. In 1879 Utes rebelled against their persecution in western Colorado, and were sharply quelled.

Elsewhere in the country the Indian resistance flared and was extinguished. In Indian Territory Satanta led the Kiowas from captivity and engaged in guerilla warfare. He was joined by the Comanches under Quanah Parker, who carried the fight across five states before both tribes were crushed and returned to the reservations. The Modocs of southern Oregon rebelled against being forced to share a reservation

The last sporadic rebellions were quelled, and the Indians slid into poverty and despair, relying on Government handouts of food (*above right*) for subsistence. Deputations of chiefs went to Washington to appeal and were turned away with hollow promises.

with the Klamath, and initiated a costly war that ended with the capture and hanging of their leader, Captain Jack, and their tribal exile to Oklahoma. The raiding Navajos were reduced by Colonel Kit Carson and locked in the barren lands of northern Arizona, while the Apaches, defeated earlier by white treachery and placed on reservations, rose against the injustices which continued to be visited on them, and scattered bands held out for many years in the rocky border country under Nachez and the legendary Geronimo. In the Northwest, the Bannocks of southern Idaho had their brief hour of revolt, and in 1877 the Nez Perces, after seventy-two years of peace, were provoked into war. Their leader, Chief Joseph, one of the greatest of all Indian heroes, made a desperate attempt to keep the peace, even agreeing to move onto a reservation. Unfortunately white settlers took the opportunity to steal several hundred of the Nez Perce's cherished horses just as the tribe was preparing to depart. Impulsive young warriors exacted instant revenge, and the troops were called out.

Joseph, once committed to war, proved himself to be as great a general as he was a statesman, and consistently out-manoeuvred the US forces. In yet another heroic Indian march he led his people for four months across a thousand miles of mountainous country in an effort to reach the safety of Canada. Engagements were fought with the pursuing army all along the route, culminating in a five-day battle in the Bear Paw Mountains and the tribe's surrender to General Miles. Joseph won high praise from his captor for the manner in which he had issued orders against scalping and captive women had been allowed to go free: 'In this skilful campaign they have spared hundreds of lives and thousands of dollars' worth of property that they might have destroyed'. Joseph made his moving speech of surrender: 'Hear me, my chiefs, I am tired; my heart is sick and sad. From where the sun now stands I will fight no more forever', and drew his blanket across his face, in the manner of Indians when mourning. So much for honour in defeat; the Nez Perces (who came from the mountains) were despatched to the malarial flatlands of the Indian Territory where Joseph's six children and a quarter of his tribe perished within a year.

The Indian cause wilted, and so did the Indian. Deputations went to Washington and returned with nothing more than their photographs. The reservations were clogged with listless people who bore the deeper scars of defeat. For the tribes who remained on the Great Plains, life was equally shorn of purpose. The buffalo had all gone, taking with them the source of their food, their shelter and their excitement. Starved of the latter, the Plains people tried the impossible. Cattle given to them by the government were hunted as if they were buffalo. But in 1890 this too was forbidden. In the same year the attempts of the Sioux to become farmers were destroyed by a bad drought. There was hunger. Their white neighbours gave up and went to live in less harsh regions, and the Sioux were reduced to living on the meagre rations doled out to them through the Bureau of Indian Affairs. It was a time of desperation, beyond hope of a practical

3564. At the Dance.
Part of 8th U.S. Cavalry and 82 Infantry at the great Indian Grass Dance on Reservation. Photo and copyright by Grabill, '90.

Prelude and aftermath to Wounded Knee.

Top right: Ghost Dance in progress.

Top left: Ghost Dancers of Big Foot's Band with US troops in the autumn of 1890. Most of the Indians in the picture were slaughtered at Wounded Knee.

Opposite: General Miles and his staff view the Indian camp two weeks after the final surrender in January 1891.

Overleaf: one of the Hotchkiss guns. The soldier seated behind it won a Medal of Honour.

solution, and they turned inward on themselves, piling their dreams.

It was a dream that brought about the last tragic revival. In 1890 news filtered through the US Postal System of a new religion, one that would restore their old world and save them from their present misery. The initiator was an Indian named Wovoka, the son of a prophet, who as a boy had been brought up in a white family as Jack Wilson. His religion combined the teachings of the two peoples, and claimed that a Messiah would come and lead the Indians back to their promised land. He had had a vision during an eclipse of the sun. The dead would rise, the buffalo would again be hunted, the whites would be driven from the continent, and the Great Spirit had given him a dance to hand on to his people.

The message of the Ghost Religion spread among the Indians like a prairie fire. They began to dance. All over the plains the tribes performed it, this Ghost Dance, with a crazed intensity that served to heighten the dream.

74

The mystical Sioux embraced it with the greatest frenzy of all, embroidering the peaceful vision of Wovoka with prophecies of grimmer aspect. They came to believe that the Ghost Shirts which they wore would protect them from the white man's bullets.

The fever of the plains disturbed the Indian agents, who feared a revival of hostilities. The Seventh Cavalry were summoned. Their presence created tension. In an unfortunate incident, the great Sioux leader, Sitting Bull was killed while being arrested, and his people purged their grief through a renewed intoxication in the Ghost Dance. A group of three hundred under Big Foot were making their way to join the main body of the tribe who were dancing in the Badlands when they were intercepted by the Cavalry. Surprisingly Big Foot's band did not resist and agreed to go peaceably with the soldiers. The Indians were wearing their Ghost Shirts.

The first night on their way back to the agency they camped in a hollow near a creek called Wounded Knee. In the morning Hotchkiss guns were lined up on the hill and cavalrymen were drawn up round the Indian encampment. The Indians were ordered to hand over their weapons. Suspicious and fearful, they refused, and in the subsequent search a shot was fired. At once the Hotchkiss guns opened up. The rapid fire and the close range meant that most of the Indians were dead within minutes. Those who fled were pursued up the creek and gunned down, including women and children. Heavy snow began to fall, and the bodies were left to freeze grotesquely where they lay. Several days later, when the storm had subsided, the dead were heaped on wagons and thrown into a mass grave. The Seventh

Cavalry were satisfied; Custer had been revenged. They were awarded twenty-six Congressional Medals of Honour for their part in the action.

The Ghost Shirts had not protected the Sioux, the religion was discredited, and the Indians were finally penned in their reservations, condemned by the futility of their history to patrol the edges of oblivion, cramped by a disillusion too complex for social panacea.

No. 3692½ Copr. Paul Wernert and gunners of Battery "E" 1st Artillery. Photo. and copyright 1891 by The Grabill P. & V. Co., Deadwood, S.D.

Gathering up the Dead at the Battle
Wounded Knee S.D.

78

After the battle.

The wounded were taken to the hospital and the Indian dead piled on wagons before being thrown into a mass grave, with soldiers covering the operation to guard against reprisals. The cavalry erected a memorial (*overleaf*) to their own dead (killed mostly by their own fire), and posed proudly beside it.

The utmost good faith shall always be observed towards the Indians; their land and property shall never be taken from them without their consent; and in their property, rights and liberty they shall never be disturbed... and lawful...

The Indian Today

It is eight decades since Wounded Knee, but the word for time does not exist in the Sioux language. It is as short or as long as they care to make it, but mostly it is without definition. Old Indians will remember that battle from their youth, and confuse it in their minds with the events of yesterday. Young Indians will be taught it as part of their past, and be confused by its relevance to their present. The memorial at that mass grave in South Dakota is as much a reminder as it is a record, for Indian history is not like white man's history, it is not labelled by dates but by moons and seasons that turn over and merge with the next. Wounded Knee was not 1890, but the moon when the Indians were told they no longer existed.

Top: the sign at the entrance to the Wounded Knee site today.

Centre: a Navajo hut in the Arizona desert which forms their reservation.

Bottom: The Badlands, part fertile, part barren, taken from the Sioux by the Government in 1942 for practice bombing runs.

They do exist, half a million of them, and exist is, for the majority, the appropriate word, living and partly living in the broken jaw of their lost kingdoms. They have shuffled into the twentieth century, reluctant to assume a mantle other than their own, and the conflict has increased within them. On the one side, the future beckons them to be assimilated in the mainstream of the Great Society; on the other, their Indian nation's pride retains them, with all its privacy and introspection. Today is a limbo; tomorrow does not come. They want to remain Indians, but the present allows them to see no future in it. The white society may solve their problems, but they see no virtue in it.

To the white man and his bureaucracy, they are the invisible people, an embarrassment by their survival. Legally, they are non-beings. To this day there is no definition of the Indian in law, or by Act of Congress. A bulletin of the Bureau of Indian Affairs produced the following: 'A person may be legally an Indian for some purposes, but not for others'. The phrase has an absurdity that extends beyond the scope of satire. It is merely typical of the official white view of the native as an irrelevant anachronism, a feeling that germinated in the national conscience a long time ago when their own history was being pioneered, that mushroomed into the legends of the West and which still, unbelievably, provides the screen fodder through which generations of young Americans formulate their *idée fixe* about these peoples. The Indians are only too aware of this, because the Hollywood myth works against them, and their own children suffer under the propaganda. They are brought up and taught to be Indians, and to be proud of being Indians, but the inevitable contact with the white man's television creates that frightened perplexity which so

often seems to be the mark of suppressed races. 'The image they are projecting through the TV Western is one where the Indian is always the sneaky guy stealing up against the good white guy. The good guy is always the one that any child wants to associate with, and the good guy is always white, a cowboy or a cavalry officer, and the bad guy is always the Indian. "The only good Indian is a dead Indian" is a cry that's still heard in this land on TV, and the child just finds it very difficult to associate with his own people, or to say, "Well, I am an Indian" after this.'

The child may find this puzzling, but adolescence will confirm it as indoctrination. Now more than ever the young Indian finds himself at odds with the world, uncertain of his destiny, and uncertain which of two destinies to choose. The one seems doomed, but is indigenous, belonging to his people; the other belongs to an alien race, is alien in itself, but may prove the more expedient. He is the modern Hamlet, but more than that. He not only contemplates suicide, too often he commits it.

The Indian suicide rate is more than three times higher than the US average in the 15–19 age group, four times higher in the 20–24 age group, and more than twice as high in the population between twenty-five and thirty-four. Statistics may cheat, but they tell heartless truths. Suicides have even been recorded among eight-year-olds. Significantly, for the group over the age of forty-five, the rate is lower than for the whole country. It reflects the gulf between the generations. The older Indian can more easily shrug off the pressures of the time because he is closer to the physical tragedies of the Indian defeat, he has long since resigned himself to what is irremediable. At the same time he can feed his pride with the conviction that he is superior to the white man

Seminole dwellings in the Florida Everglades, virtually unchanged since the time the tribe held out there more than a hundred years ago.

The image of the Indian projected through the cinema screen has been predominantly one of a cunning savage given to wanton acts of barbarity. Equally, as played by white men, the character portrayals have seldom risen above the level of unfortunate caricature.

and therefore prefers to remain separate. The younger generation are not so fortunate. The forces which besiege them are part of a subtler genocide. They face two futures, both without hope. Their despair drives them to suicide, and the lack of excitement in their lives encourages them further to embrace the act as a kind of dare-devilry. They see, too, their elders dying from the slow death of alcoholism and this taunts them with its grim prophecy, for many are themselves early committed to drink. Boys get drunk and play Russian Roulette, careless of their fate but determined to prove they

are not cowards. The psychological effects of their defeat before the white man lead them to create the illusion that they are worthy of the inherited Indian pride. They dare not be afraid.

In the old days suicide, though rare, was part of the social pattern. If you had committed a wrong, or your family had, then it was the proper thing for someone to take their life and thus redeem their family in the eyes of the community. Suicide pacts were also not unusual. The attitude of the Indian society was one of acceptance, and it does not greatly differ today. They feel that it serves a point, that the

The young Indians today are torn between two cultures, unable to reconcile themselves either to the misery of their people (*overleaf*) or to the materialism of the American society.

person was lost and has found himself. It is the reasons for suicide that have changed. 'When the old Indian world collapsed, the Indian man was destroyed. The old Indian world was a man's world. There was no question about it. The ideal was that a warrior hunted, and the woman, whether she was wife or mother or daughter, took glory in her son or her husband or her father. This was the important thing. So that when the old world was destroyed, when the buffalo were wiped out, you couldn't hunt, they were locked up on the reservations, there was no possibility of encounter with the enemy. There was no reason for the Indian man to go on living. So the blow to the male ego was far

greater than most people have ever realized.'

The ego was damaged, and the frustrations built up as the modern white world reached into the reservations. The Indian's contact with the big cities caused him to pick up the American values of whatever branch of the community he mixed with. He was attempting to better himself, and if his habits and his behaviour did not meet with the demands of a white society, he could find no companionship. He became confused about what he should be, how he should behave and appear to others. The suicide attempts of the girls on the reservations relate particularly to the influence of the cities. They depend to the same degree on pills and

borrow the disillusion that relies on artificial remedies, forgetting the traditional Indian gift of philosophical detachment. Their suicide rate is higher, and has nothing to do with whether they are pretty or not. There are instances of talented and attractive girls taking their life through the same universal despair, unable to equate the slum cultures of the American cities with the culture they have been taught their people once had but which they are no longer allowed to practise. In this respect education

and intelligence are often a handicap. At school the child may be struggling against all sorts of odds to establish herself; she goes home for the weekend or for the vacation; her parents drink and are alien to her in their own despair. The sense of failure and disenchantment seeps through, creating the vacuum that is filled by frustration. It is in this tense atmosphere that most of the suicide attempts occur, at home on the reservations rather than at school.

Violence has also come to the reservations from the cities, creating a different dissension. Contrary to the contorted picture of their history that is handed out through the popular media, the Indians are a gentle people. Even those tribes that demonstrated the greatest hostility in the wars with the white man had an abstracted sympathy and an understanding that was part of their relationship with their environment. They were the perfect human products of that environment, as much a component of it as was the buffalo, and they were deeply conscious of their place in this visible universe. It was a world that embraced them as one with the elements of land, sea and sky, and with the other creatures of nature. It bred in them, too, their strong sense of community and their attitudes towards each other, their reverence for the whole human personality. The recurrent persecutions served to drive them closer together for as long as they remained unified, but when the white man's society encroached and divided them, their communion with each other was broken. Feeling that they had to establish a harmony with their 'civilizers', they found themselves adopting the habits that would endear them to the white community. Consequently they picked up ways that conflicted with their Indianness. Violence is one of them, and, as with the suicides, it has become a vicious web from which they cannot break.

Violence, death, the creeping paralysis of alcohol. It might apply to any period of Indian history from the time of the white man's arrival. The perpetuity of these things today, together with

the modern social vices of unemployment an frustration, create a picture that is more trag than any episode from their past because it unequivocally bleak. The Removals, the Trail Tears, the Sand Creek Massacre, the smallpo epidemics were more specific catastrophes, b up until Wounded Knee there was always t possibility of hope, until the final round-u there was room for the dreams of revival. Th mystics inhabited their grassy plains, the cav dwellers their arid heights. Today they a lumped together in the desolate encampmen known as reservations, which were created a temporary measure and which have becom their permanent resting-places. In appearan some of them are little better than concentr tion camps, and the bleakness is implicit in th —areas of waste land dotted by shacks and su rounded by wire. Even the most fulsome esta agent would find it difficult to describe the winningly. They are without definition, wit out charm, without serenity, vacant spac peopled by dogs, chickens, battered cars an the residue of the first Americans. Violen and alcoholism seem natural to this landscape.

The reservations are the homes of a natic defeated by the United States, and in th respect the Indians have been less generous treated than either of the two other majc nations conquered by that country. Unlik Japan or Germany, no great sums of mone have been spent on their rehabilitation. In fa their situation worsened after their defea General Sherman once asked the questic 'What is an Indian Reservation?' and th answer was 'An Indian Reservation is a parc of land set aside for Indians, surrounded k thieves'. The statistics prove that reply is st valid. Out of the 138 million acres that ha been the Indians' in 1887, only 56 million acr remained in 1934. Of those the Bureau Indian Affairs estimated that fourteen millic acres were 'critically eroded', and not one ac was considered 'uneroded'. Nevertheless, th BIA, in its wisdom, decided that the Indians c reservations should become agriculturalis even though most of them, by tradition, ar not. It even tried to change the fishing com munities into farmers. It was another kind robbery, and typical of the over-protectiv attitude that has been predominant in govern mental handling of the Indians.

Paternalism may be a dirty word in India Affairs, but it still exists, born of the criminal guilt, characterized by over-zealousness i theory and shortsightedness in practice. N American Administration of the twentiet century can look back on its dealings with th Indians without a blush, however sonorou and well-meaning its intentions. The proposa of individual idealists have always been crippl by the faceless machine of the bureaucracy whose conclusion has generally been that it easier to do the job itself than teach a bunch ignorant Indians how to do it. In additio bribery, corruption, graft and incompetenc have frustrated the efforts to improve the lc of the native. It is not without significance tha from the time of George Washington's Pre sidency until 1849 the administration of India Affairs was directed by the War Departmen When the BIA was established its purpose wa to deal with a defeated enemy. The policy coercive cultural change began, determined t

'They were beggars. They were paupers. They came to this country looking for freedom of speech and to worship the way they wanted to. But when they got here they forgot when it came to the Indian. This country is built on total aggression.'

make shadows of a people who could not be respected for having been defeated, who must be misguided for having been an enemy. A BIA superintendent offered the cynical explanation – 'In history the US government discovered that it was cheaper to keep them on the reservations than to try and kill them. So they were marched into what we hoped were useless pieces of land.' They were usually right in their assessment of the latter, and once the Indians had been confined, reduced to dependence on charity, the BIA could control their future.

The thinking behind the BIA's actions is that the reservations are in fact temporary, and that the Indian will eventually disappear into the American mainstream. It meets with resistance. 'The white people who are trying to

tradition, are democratically controlled an[d] not wealth controlled. In any case they have n[o] faith in white bureaucracy. Scarcely any legis[la]lation passed proves of ultimate benefit to th[e] Indians. The distribution of federal funds [is] subject to the worst examples of graft an[d] expropriation. There are BIA workers who ar[e] quite open about their motives in working fo[r] the agency, their attitude being that they woul[d] not dream of spending their days in the wilder[-]ness of the reservations if they could not ge[t] something out of it for themselves. In additio[n] it is rare to find a Bureau worker on a reserva[-]tion who can speak a word of the nativ[e] language, or who is properly trained in medicin[e] or teaching. It is impossible not to recall th[e] behaviour of the agents during the enforce[d]

An Indian couple on a 'flatcar', a remnant of nineteenth-century rural America. No white farmer uses anything but lorries.

make us over into their image, they want us to be what they call assimilated, bringing the Indians into the mainstream and destroying our own way of life and our own cultural patterns. They believe that we should be contented to become like those whose concept of happiness is two cars and a colour TV, a very materialistic and greedy society which is very different from our way.'

The implacable misunderstanding continues. The BIA has persistently failed to understand what the Indian has wanted and has always applied what it thought the Indian needed. The result is that it is regarded with resentment and equivocation by the native, who remains suspicious of its intentions. In particular, any step towards termination of the reservations is violently opposed. Living separately they can preserve their own detachment, and run their own tribal societies which, true to the Indian

removals in the 1830s. Then, as now, fund[s] often did not reach their destination or wer[e] used for the wrong purposes. Even today th[e] government persist with cash handouts whic[h] are not tied to any programme and which mee[t] with the expected fate. Rash spending on drink[,] cars and fancy goods eat through the funds i[n] no time, and the Indians return to the welfar[e] roll, their new Cadillac rotting outside with a[n] empty gas tank. The Menominee Indians [of] Wisconsin were given a million dollars in 196[ ] and told to find their own way in the world[.] They are now worse off than ever. Meanwhil[e] the white traders have closed in like vulture[s] and taken their pickings from the simple[,] gullible people for whom money, legal con[-]tracts, hire purchase are beyond understandin[g] and who for centuries existed without them.

When so much has been written about th[e] Indians and their way of life, the continuin[g]

This page and overleaf: nearly 400,000 Indians live on reservations, and their living conditions are pitiful. All but a few inhabit shacks such as these, often without running water. Their families are large, their mortality rate high.

myopia of the BIA, as expressed by their actions, defies belief. As in Vietnam, the situation has escalated from a conflict of cultures into a roundabout from which nobody dares jump off, and which will continue to rotate in ever more meaningless circles. Similarly there is a parallel to be found between the original Indian and Oriental cultures, both of which are based on a detached and gentle mysticism outside the experience of most of the materialists who seek to change them. Even if understood by them, any kind of involvement leads to actions which warp if they do not destroy. The motivations of white society—power, prestige, money, comfort—and their resulting side-effects—hostility, fear, envy, jealousy—are the opposites of the Indian way, and yet they are pursued by the bodies responsible for the Indian welfare.

Once upon a time the Indians were amused by the white man's ways. George Catlin, the painter, who travelled extensively among the Indian tribes and often lived with them, described a dialectic that he had with a Sioux chief on the virtues of their respective civilizations. The Sioux told him that 'he had often heard that white people hung their criminals by the neck and choked them to death like dogs, and those their own people; to which I answered, "yes". He then told me he had learned that they shut each other up in prisons, where they keep them a great part of their lives because they can't pay money! I replied in the affirmative to this, which occasioned great surprise and excessive laughter, even amongst the women. He told me that he had been to our Fort, at Council Bluffs, where we had a great many warriors and braves, and he saw three of them taken out on the prairies and tied to a post and whipped almost to death, and he had been told that they submit to all this to get a little money. He said...that he had been along the frontier, and a good deal amongst the white people, and he had seen them whip their little children—a thing that was very cruel... He put me a chapter of other questions, as to the trespasses of the white people on their lands—their continual corruption of the morals of their women—and digging open the Indians' graves to get their bones, etc. To all of which I was compelled to reply in the affirmative, and quite glad to close my notebook, and quietly to escape from the throng that had collected around me, and saying (though to myself and silently) that these and a hundred other vices belong to the civilized world, and are practised upon (but certainly, in no instance, reciprocated by) the "cruel and relentless savage".'

The Indians soon learned through bitter experience that the ways of the white man were something other than amusing. In 1886, fifty years after Catlin's discomfiture, another Sioux, Black Elk, journeyed to Chicago and New York with a 'Wild West Show', in an effort to learn something that would help his people. 'I did not see anything to help my people. I could see that the Wasichus (white men) did not care for each other the way our people did before the nation's hoop was broken. They would take everything from each other if they could, and so there were some who had more of everything than they could use, while crowds of people had nothing at all and maybe were starving. They had forgotten that the earth was their mother. This could not be better than the old

When the Indian was defeated he was driven on to the land that the white man did not want. The only tribes to benefit were those consigned to territory concealing unsuspected oil or mineral deposits.

ways of my people. There was a prisoner's house on an island where the big water came up to the town, and we saw that one day. Men pointed guns at the prisoners and made them move around like animals in a cage. This made me feel very sad, because my people too were penned up in islands, and maybe that was the way the Wasichus were going to treat them.'

The earth was their mother, and that is forgotten. They are tied by the invisible bond to the land and whether it be the barren waste of Arizona or the endless sky of the Dakotas the relationship is the same. Those who seek to close the reservations and push them into the urban maelstrom may be prompted by their own standards of living, but they do not remember where the Indian has his roots. These people will have seen the condition of the reservations, the housing, the sanitation, the obdurate soil, and will think without prejudice that such places are unfit for human habitation. But, as the Indians see it, the remedy lies in improvement of these conditions. To close the reservations would be to take all that they have, for they are, as someone has said, 'those portions of land which are still retained by the Indian'; and the land was what they originally owned and for which they reserved their special reverence. Even though they may suffer from discrimination and oppression living as they do, it seems to them that it would be infinitely more perilous to venture outside to the urban jailhouse of the Great Society, disowned from their land and their tribal values. Their existence may now be a veil of intrinsic sadness, but it retains the Indian timelessness, bound by the revolving moons. Away from the earth are the white man's inventions, time and its measurers, and the white man's diseases that split the mind in two, and from which their own children are now suffering.

The reservations are the land that the Indian holds, but still he has to fend off the attempts to take what he has. The way in which history repeats itself in this respect is almost compulsive, the greed of the white man snowballing with his guilt. It is as though he must purge his conscience by removing all visible traces of the stain that blots it. William Carlos Williams felt the obsession of the settlers to justify their claim to the whole continent: 'The land! don't you feel it. Doesn't it make you want to go out and lift dead Indians tenderly from their graves, to steal from them — as if it must be clinging even to their corpses—some authenticity...' Their land is stolen, and their rights are taken away by the infernal processes of white man's law. This applies particularly to the hunting and fishing rights on which many Indians depend entirely, in the same way that the Plains Indians once lived by the buffalo.

The fishing dispute in Washington State has dragged on for fifteen years or more, with nothing resolved. It has become a yardstick by which discrimination against the Indians can be measured, both now and in the past, and it goes back into the past for its origins. Before the Europeans arrived the natives of the North west coast were the richest people in North America. They were among the few hunting fishing and gathering societies which produced wealth beyond what was needed for subsistence

With their husbands poorly paid or out of work, the Indian women struggle to feed their families. Some rely on their own enterprises, such as preserve-making or the weaving of baskets.

Overleaf: **from behind wire fences . . .**

But fishing was the central activity in their lives, for they were aware of the nature of the great watershed which surrounded them. They called themselves after the river in which they fished, and were knit together by this fact. 'Our people were fisher people and had been for thousands and thousands of years. The same as there were buffalo people—they depended on the buffalo for their way of life—our people was fishing. They had a highly developed fishing culture, and this was so deeply a way of life to them that they weren't concerned about the land—only about being allowed to go free to pursue their fishing activities.'

When Governor Stevens forced them to sign the Treaty of Medicine Creek in 1854 they were assigned to reservations but retained the right, under the Treaty, 'of taking fish at all usual and accustomed places, together with the privilege of hunting, gathering roots and berries and pasturing their horses on open and unclaimed lands.' As with most of the treaties made between white man and Indian, it was written to last for as long as 'the grass grows and the sun comes up in the east and sets in the west', and as with most of the treaties it has been broken by the white man in the cause of 'progress'.

The Indians of Washington State suffer from a continuous malevolent pressure over the fishing rights. They have watched their lands diminish since the time of Medicine Creek—the Puyallups now own only thirty-three acres of land, the Nisqually two acres, the Snohomish sixteen, while the Muckleshoot tribe of three hundred members share a reservation of a quarter of an acre. Deprived of their land and depending on fish for their livelihood, they have been forced to fish off the reservation. According to the treaty this is perfectly within their rights, but the State has laid claim to the off-reservation waters, knowing full well the money to be made from the rivers teeming with steelhead trout and the Pacific Salmon who come back to spawn. The white arguments rely on the theory of conservation, and they enforce them by pressurizing the Indians, confiscating their boats and their nets, and taking them to court.

The Indians at Frank's Landing have been arrested consistently over a period of years. Each time their fishing gear is confiscated, and a new round of litigation starts, sometimes ending in a prison sentence. Going to court has become part of the cycle of their lives. They go dressed defiantly as Indians, even though long hair for men was forbidden by a government order in the later part of the last century, and even though it provokes an irrational fury among the Game and Fisheries Wardens. But by their determination, they have succeeded in placing their problem in the public eye. They staged a demonstration at Frank's Landing. 'We said that we were going to demonstrate this right by going out and going fishing, which we feel is a passive way of resisting this force used against us. The State came down in a large force of about fifty Game and Fisheries Wardens, to put down a group of about eight adults and about thirty children, ranging from two years old on to seventeen.' The scene developed into an ugly maul in which the Indians claim (and this is supported by photographic evidence) they were manhandled with billy clubs, and

their women and children kicked and punched. A court case resulted, and for once the Indians did not suffer from a discriminatory verdict. What did emerge to the general public was that the behaviour of the State officials towards these Indians had been shabby in the extreme, and often brutal. Their pious postures of innocence with regard to their dealings with the natives were exposed, and the Indians won a minor victory.

It has not helped them greatly. They still suffer from the pressure and the discrimination. Legally they cannot hope to win many other cases, because technically they do not exist. A white lawyer involved in the dispute has said that one could read the State Fishery Laws from beginning to end and find no mention of Indians. And most of the litigation stems from the question of conservation. In this, white man and Indian differ sharply over the inter-

pretation of what constitutes conservation. To the Indians it is their natural way, as with every thing they hunt and catch. 'The Indian never had to conserve. This was done automatically by the Indian. They never kill anything they can't use. They never kill for sport, they never fish for the sport of it. Fishing to us is a livelihood. We never take anything we can't use. This is conservation to us.' To the white man at the most cynical level, conservation mean preventing the Indian from fishing when the river is full of fish, and in particular when the Pacific Salmon return upstream. The Indians are entitled to be scathing—'They want us to give up our way of life to make room for the spor and pleasure of a kind of decadent society. They want it for a sportsman's paradise. They advertise nationwide ''Come to Washington a sportsman's wonderland''—and the Indian make wry jokes about the State of Washington

The Indians of Washington State depend on the fishing for their livelihood. For years they have suffered from commercial and legal pressures to prevent them fishing for the Pacific salmon and the steelhead trout that come up river to spawn.

decreeing that the steelhead trout is a 'white man's fish', wondering if perhaps the white men think the steelhead swam over behind the Mayflower. But their anger simmers beneath at the constant infringements on their freedom. 'Now you have to have permission to gather nuts and things from the mountains and from the desert. They didn't plant these trees here. They didn't bring the deer here. They didn't bring the fish here, and yet they say: "We give you—we give you the right to fish here—we give you". They had nothing to give in the first place. They were beggars, they were paupers. They came to this country looking for freedom of speech and to worship the way they wanted to. But when they got here they forgot when it came to the Indian. This country is built on total aggression. There was room for everyone. But now he owns everything and now he wants to take the rest of us—he wants

to take away everything we have. They've taken our religion. They've taken our identity. They've taken everything.'

The comments of those Indians who have returned to Washington State after service in Vietnam are particularly bitter. They feel that they have served the United States in a less compelling struggle in Southeast Asia and refuse to be restricted from doing the same, using passive methods, for their own people within the United States. One sergeant is back in Vietnam on his third tour of duty. During the course of his service there he has been awarded a Silver Star and a Bronze Star, but while home on furlough, recovering from combat wounds and attempting to provide for his large family, he was arrested three times in one month for illegal net fishing. As another member of his tribe put it, 'the US would have accepted sacrifice of his life in Vietnam in a less legitimate

'They want us to give up
our way of life to make
room for the sport and
pleasure of a kind of
decadent society. They
want it for a sportsman's
paradise. They advertise
nationwide "Come to
Washington, a sports-
man's wonderland".'

106

'The white man, he took over, see, after he saw there was money in fish. He just took over, you know, just steal – like stealing off the Indian. And that's how they got it. And that's why they don't want the Indian to fish, because there's big money for them. Indian is nothing to the white man. He's nothing.'

'The Indian never had to conserve. This was done automatically by the Indian. They never kill anything they can't use. They never kill for sport, they never fish for the sport of it. Fishing to us is a livelihood.'

cause, in fact would have honoured such a death, but for fighting for his family and people they permitted a professional barber acting as a Justice of the Peace to interpret his treaty, to ignore his right, to impose punishment, and to record a criminal conviction'.

The Washington State fishing controversy is the Indian-white conflict in a nutshell, both now and in the past. Their history breathes back at them, soured by injustice. The speech that Chief Sealth made at the Medicine Cre Treaty in 1854 could have been written f today: '...and when the last Red Man sh have perished, and the memory of my tri shall have become a myth among the Whi Men, these shores will swarm with the invisib dead of my tribe, and when your childrer children think themselves alone in the fiel the store, the shop, upon the highway, or the silence of the pathless woods, they will n

be alone... At night when the streets of your cities and villages are silent and you think them deserted, they will throng with the returning hosts that once filled and still love this beautiful land. The White Man will never be alone.'

The white man will never be alone, the Indian will never be left alone. The case of the Badlands and the Oglala Sioux in the Dakotas is a modern parallel of so many incidents in their past. In 1942 the US Government found itself urgently in need of ground to train pilots on practice bombing runs. They selected an area of 500 square miles in the Badlands as being the most suitable. Half of this area was barren, and the other half was rich grazing land, but all of it belonged to the Oglala Sioux. The Government moved swiftly to obtain it, informing the Indians that it was a wartime state of emergency, that if they stayed on the land they would either be bombed or they

The Indian child inherits an affinity to the land and to nature. It is destroyed if he is relocated to the urban community. It is destroyed if he is prevented from hunting and fishing on his own territory.

would be killed by the Japs 'who were just over the hill'. Some of the Indians were given as little as eight days' notice to remove themselves, and none of them had more than a month's grace. It was an instant eviction, achieved by a lie and by the promises that they would be refunded the value of their land and could return to it as soon as the emergency was over. As to the first promise, the Indians received miserable reward. One man who owned 320 acres was paid $232 for it, and was ordered to move so quickly that he was forced to leave his horses and cattle behind–'we left them, we took our bedding and things in the

the Indians started to graze their cattle on the land they found that they had to lease it from the War Department. By now some of them have paid back in rent three or four times the amount they originally received for the land. Theoretically they would be allowed to buy it back for the same price they were paid, plus interest for the 'improvement' of the land. If the land has improved at all, it is because the Sioux have been leasing it to graze cattle; it can scarcely have done so while being used for bombing practice. But the felony has been worse compounded by the action of the War Department who in 1965, unknown to the

Overleaf: Navajo's revenge.

Indian girls in a mission school. Their dresses are second hand, donated, and worn for big occasions only.

wagon, and came out here, and those horses and cattle are still out there. Maybe they died of age or maybe they used them for target practice. I don't know what...' When his family were relocated in another part of the reservation, they owned nothing and had to pay to live on the land to which they were moved. Another woman was offered $200 for 400 acres. She protested that it was not enough, but was coerced into signing by appeals to her patriotic sentiments. Land belonging to Indians who could not be traced was condemned by the War Department and taken over.

If there is excuse for this in the crisis of war, there is none for the failure to carry out the second promise. The Sioux who were removed have still not returned, though the emergency ended twenty-five years ago. When, at the end of the war, the tribe inquired about regaining possession of their land, they were told that the leases they held were worthless, and that the officials who promised them in the first place that their land would be returned to them had no authority to do so. The white man wriggled out because there was nothing in writing. When

tribe, declared the land surplus and handed it over to the General Services administration. The Federal Park Service laid claim to the waste ground in the hope of annexing it to the Badlands National Monument, and South Dakota cattle interests aimed at grabbing the rich grasslands at bargain prices. The Indians are helpless because the buying and selling of their land is controlled by the Bureau of Indian Affairs, and by that very token they see little hope of their property ever returning to them.

Cajole, bribe, threaten, confuse by litigation. The white man's trickery continues. The Indian knows his word cannot be trusted, but has to exist on his charity, for which the Indian is obliged to show gratitude. But the charity is often hollow, worse than active malevolence because less honest. How can they learn to help themselves in their dealings with the whites without compromising their Indianness? As yet they lack that kind of sophistication.

Education is perhaps the most critical problem. 'The Indian child coming to school is

usually not going to have the motivation given to him by his parents. Schools, for example, are one of the things that Indian people look on as something that's been brought in by the white man. It's something like TB and some of the other evils that have come along. So that first of all the child doesn't have the appreciation or desire for success in school that the average non-Indian child is going to have when he goes. But when he comes he usually finds it very interesting. He is attracted by it and by tests we find that, while at the start he will fall below the norms of the national education tests, as he moves up to the 2nd, 3rd, 4th and 5th grades, he not only achieves the norms, b will over-achieve. He will go higher than t average child taking the test. Then we fi when they reach the junior-high level, a gradu decline in his showing in the tests, and if t child is going to decline he will fall farther a farther below the national norms as each ye goes on. What is happening of course, is t child at this age realizes that he is an India He realizes also that all his training, his educ tion, has directed him to non-Indian values, h directed him off the reservation. This is a tir when frustration takes place. It's a ba psychological problem.'

The Indians have never liked the idea of schools, as the 1899 picture on this page illustrates. Today many of them recognize that education is the only way in which they will be able to compete, but the schooling system creates disastrous problems for the young.

The Indians face the same conflict of values as the Five Civilized Tribes felt a hundred and fifty years ago when the radical innovations of white society broke their tribal unity. While they know that they must encourage the education of their children in order to give them a chance of competing, the Indians also know that this is the cause of their children's instability in adolescence, and of the frightening suicide rate. Because of the nature of their education, the majority are instructed in priorities that conflict with the ways of their own people. In addition nearly sixty per cent of the children have to attend BIA boarding schools, and this has a particularly destructive impact on the family system of the Indians, especially among those tribes, like the Hopi and the Navajo, who have preserved their tribal structure to a high degree. Many are separated from their families before they are five years old, because there is no public or federal day school near their homes. Others are sent to boarding school because, according to the BIA, they are 'social referrals', which can mean anything from a bilingual difficulty to serious emotional disorders and juvenile delinquency. The effects are predictable. One per cent of the Indians in college complete the course.

Among the Navajo who constitute a third of the total Indian population, ninety-two per cent of the children are in BIA boarding schools; a sixty per cent dropout rate is recorded. On average, Indians complete only five years schooling.

The BIA educational policy frustrates at two levels. Most Indian children come to school speaking English poorly or not at all, creating difficulties of communication between teacher and pupil. Yet the Bureau insist that their schools conduct all classes in English. The turnover rate among teachers is, not surprisingly, double the national average. The problem of recruitment is not helped by the fact of only one per cent of the Indians graduating from college. Again it is a vicious circle, but there might be some hope of a practical solution if the educational aims of the BIA were not so misguided. The policy of assimilation is directed towards the Indians at the earliest possible age, thereby implying that a change of culture is synonymous with education. Thus it suits the Bureau that the children in boarding schools are far from their homes and divorced from their native environments. In this respect they are

misery. The Indian child in a boarding school is separated from his family, often unable to communicate at all with his teachers, and indoctrinated with a culture that is not only foreign to him but which his own parents do not embrace. He is likewise subject to the extraordinary system of promotion which works in the schools, whereby the child is automatically promoted to the next grade at the end of the academic year without any regard to intelligence or performance. The classes are consequently filled with pupils of hopelessly divergent ability. The Indians are taught the standard subjects, these including ancient history, European history and American history, but nothing of their own history except where it coincides with the white man's. Instilled at home with the significance of their cultural heritage, they learn nothing of it in the classroom. Their extra-curricular activities are regimented, and their dress regulated as they are discouraged from wearing any of the elaborate personal decorations traditional to their peoples. Most BIA schools do not teach the Indian languages, and not so long ago there was flagrant discrimination against Indians

The children generally do well early on but fall away later when they realize they have been educated away from their Indianness.

especially successful in Alaska, where there is only one federal high school, so more than two-thirds of the Alaskan Indians are sent to boarding schools in Oregon and Oklahoma.

Many Indians, with their strong family traditions, resist having their children sent away. In a recent survey it was estimated that sixteen thousand Indian children between the ages of eight and sixteen were not in school. At the same time more than nine thousand under the age of nine were away in boarding establishments. It produces a picture of bankrupt

speaking their own language amongst themselves. The result of all this is that many try to run away, others resort to drink, and the extreme cases take their own lives.

Nearly 400,000 Indians live on reservations. The others have either been fully assimilated into the American society, or have been resettled in urban areas under the relocation policy of the BIA. This runs in parallel with their termination policy, and is equally at variance with the

GRADUATION

Graduation exercises began with Father Emmett Hoffmann, O.F.M. Cap. offering the Holy Sacrifice of Mass for the graduates on the evening of May 18th. Relatives, friends and the entire student body participated to honor the seventeen high school and the nineteen grade school graduates.

HIGH SCHOOL GRADUATES

Phyllis Bearcomesout
Robert Bement
Gilbert Brady
Darrell Brightwings
Henry Brightwings
Wesley Crooked Arm
Mark Elkshoulder
Richard M. Fisher

Richard L. Fisher
Amy Foote
Dennis Limberhand
Georgiann Littlehead
Larry Redwoman
Jocelyn Rowland
Thomas Trusler
James Walkslast

Winslow Whitecrane

GRADE SCHOOL GRADUATES

George Bement
Mary Ann Bighead
Edwin Biglefthand
Wreatha Blackwolf
Delpha Eaglefeathers
George Elkshoulder
Charles Evans
Ruth Falls Down
Francine Fisher

Francis Fisher
Arlene Gliko
Perry Redwoman
Annabelle Rowland
Donald Rowland
Emmanuel Seminole
Charlotte Strange Owl
Orville Two Bulls
Billy Two Moons

Frances Whiteman

Even if the child is comparatively happy at school he is likely to be afflicted by doubts and confusion when he goes home to the reservation (*overleaf*), which is one of the reasons why so few complete more than a few years of schooling.

Georgiann Littlehead, Valedictorian

James Walkslast, Salutatorian

native instinct. The Indians, having had a whole continent wrested from them, are now either too numerous for the territories assigned them by the government, or the land is too inferior to support them. The Bureau, if it is not to terminate the reservations, finds itself faced with the alternative of relocating the surplus population. A third alternative is the enlargement of the tribal domains but that would be running against the tide of history, and would in itself be an admission of national guilt.

At present, however, termination is opposed, and relocation produces unhappy results. Relocated Indians, even of mature years, find the transition from the reservation to the big city perilous, one that requires all kinds of adjustments beyond the fact of a rural worker moving to an urban setting. That in itself may create tension, but to migrate from a tribal society into the spiritless heart of a materialist community involves a re-alignment of standards and values that strikes at the very root of their Indianness. In addition, the federal government appears to be concerned

The problems of employment are severe. The majority of Indians are unhappy in the big cities, and there is little work to be found on the reservations. The Indians on these pages are more fortunate. The ideal is to be able to work on the land and feed themselves off it (*overleaf*).

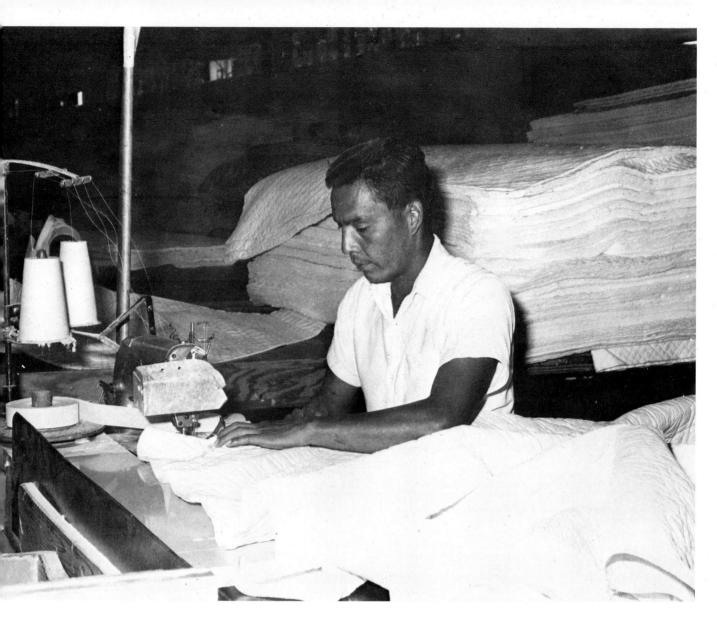

only with their initial employment and housing arrangements. After that they must sink or swim on their own. The greater number sink, falling into alcoholism and beggary. The discrimination, both economic and social, the urban culture, the substandard housing, and their own lack of education defeat all but the most resilient and frustrate them in their original purpose, which was simply to earn a living and support their families. 'The white man is trying to get all of us to leave the reservation and go to the city, and I can go to the city of Seattle right now and I can find you Indians by the thousands on Skid Row up there and now they don't own nothing. Nobody wants them. They're nothing but bums.' The relocated Indians are seen as deserters who have abdicated their tribal responsibilities by those who have stayed on the reservations and who have fought against the contamination of their relationship with the earth.

For those Indians without access to hunting or fishing grounds and who want to stay on the reservations, there is the bleak problem of employment. 'There is nothing. The farming communities have become highly mechanized and don't need the Indians as they used to, so it's hard to exist. The Indian income is not only low income. I'd say low income would be high,

but they are no income people. They have no way of supporting themselves. The whites, they tell you to go out and live and get a job just like anybody else, but the unions are generally closed. In fact, one Indian just recently here, the VISTA workers filled an application for this Indian to a union. Just as soon as they found out that he was an Indian, they turned thumbs down on him, and if you can't join a union in this state you can't get a job, and then they tell you you can't get a job unless you belong to the union. And this is just a gimmick they use with the Indians.' The discrimination has worked at a higher level too. Most of the reservations are miles away from a town of any size, and the federal government has done little to create any kind of employment for the Indians on, or near, their own land. The Indians who go to the cities are generally those who can find no work, who are either unable to support their families or are totally demoralized by their aimless existence, and who feel that any kind of change would be preferable to that. The fact that many return to the reservations, to the prospect of no employment, underlines more than anything the Indian's feeling for his own kind, and the horror with which he views the remoteness and self-interest of the urban populace.

The government agencies have in recent

years been heard to congratulate themselves on the improvements they have brought about in Indian housing, income, health and employment. It is true that over the past ten years living conditions have been perceptibly raised. But, compared with the white man's society, the general state of the Indian today makes this official self-satisfaction positively laughable. In most tribes the unemployment figures waver between forty and eighty per cent, particularly in the winter when there is no casual labour to be had. In some they have been as high as ninety per cent, and the majority of those in work

who survived birth, one third would die in the first year of life of 'preventable diseases'. Reservation Indians have a death rate from tuberculosis that is 400 per cent higher than that of the white population, from pneumonia and influenza that is 300 per cent higher. The white diseases still decimate the tribes; it is almost as though they have resisted acquiring resistance against them. Hepatitis and meningitis are widespread, as are venereal disease and dysentery. Trachoma exists in the United States only on the Indian reservations. On one of these it has been estimated that sixty-one per cent of

This page: medical aid on the reservations is 'periodical'. This, combined with their general living conditions, means that the standard of Indian health is terribly low.

Opposite: Indians have shown that they have a capacity for work that requires patience and delicate attention to detail.

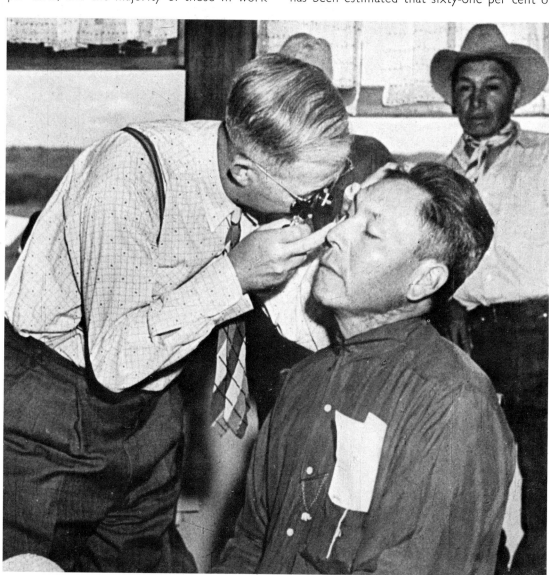

have been employed in their own tribal administrations. Where income is concerned, the average Indian wage is $30 a week, compared with the white and black population for whom the average is $130 a week. Some Indians exist on just a few hundred dollars a year. As for living conditions, ninety per cent live in shacks and sixty per cent have no running water. With large families, often as many as eleven or twelve, inhabiting such hovels, the sickness and mortality rates are predictably high—the average age of death is forty-four years, and in regions of large Indian populations such as Arizona and Alaska it is averaged in the early thirties. Among infants, the mortality rate is twice that of the general population, and one survey calculated that, of those Indian infants

the children between five and eighteen years are afflicted, are therefore either blind or going blind. The incidence of throat and middle-ear infections is likewise staggering. On some reservations a quarter of the children are deaf. Malnutrition is, not surprisingly, commonplace.

In the face of these figures, it needs a generous disposition to believe that the government are not still committed to the idea of extermination. Their medical care is spread so thin, their allotment of funds so inefficiently channelled, and their welfare policies so mismanaged, that they might almost be thought to be working on the theory of 'if we can't get them to join us, we'll beat them'. Much of the money poured into welfare programmes ends up in white pockets, doing nothing to alleviate Indian poverty. Scarcely any factories are opened on reservations to provide employment; the funds allocated go towards such small concerns as service stations and taverns, run, or controlled, by white men. This in itself is a negation of the ability of the Indians to carry out many kinds of work at which they are more skilful than the whites. They are renowned for their patience and their attention to detail and are able to perform jobs that require intricate manual dexterity. Businesses that demand this sort of work would provide employment, which would in turn enable the Indians to help themselves,

half centuries, this power survives. It is the Indian gift, which they inherited from their lost world of perfection and which they have retained by means of that same regenerative thread which keeps them separate from the white man and true to their race.

If this has relevance to their predicament today, it lies in the fact that they can transcend the conflicts which they face. Their society has virtues which they know to be superior to any that may be imposed upon them. Detachment and introspection, the scale of values that begins and ends with what is ideologically important,

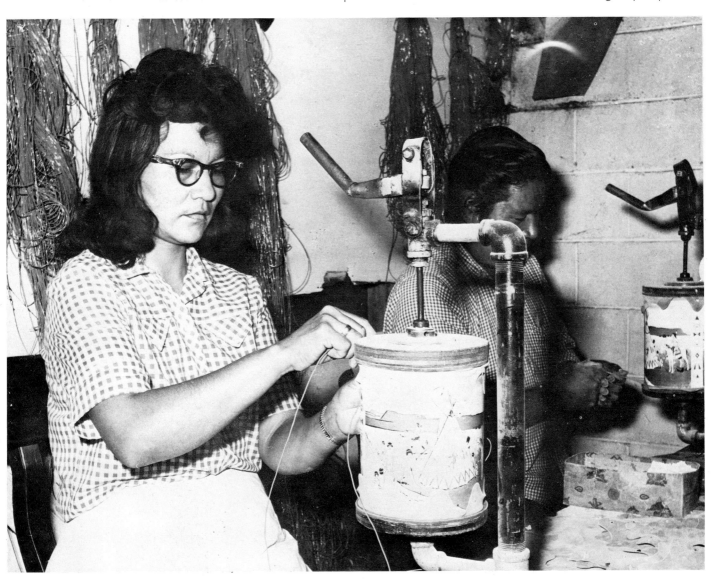

to improve their living conditions and to remain on the reservations. Sadly such opportunities are few and far between. The government, eager to assimilate, encourages them to work away from their peoples. Thus the policy of integration has a double edge to it, ensuring as it does that those on reservations will continue to be wedded to a barren existence.

The Indians knew the meaning of society long before the white man came. They knew and had the power of living, creatively, forcefully, compassionately, together in the ideal sense which the white man has always sought and failed to achieve. Incredibly, in spite of the sentences of death passed on their communities over four and a

are what they have always had and what they have preserved through their dark journey. In a political sense it affords no solution to their problems; in a practical sense it can give them the spiritual certainty that ignores pain. John Collier, who was Commissioner of Indian Affairs from 1933 to 1945, has written of the Indian way: 'Self-willed, self-wrought personality excellence, empowered by the whole social institution of the tribe and of the race, is more than a merely practical thing, according to their answer—according to their view of selfhood, society and the wide world. It is the very essence of cosmic survival and victory.

'As we traverse Indian history from the Conquest down to their present-day strivings, and up and down the two continents, we come

'The white man is trying to get all of us to leave the reservation and go to the city, and I can go to the city of Seattle right now and I can find you Indians by the thousands on Skid Row up there and now they don't own nothing. Nobody wants them.'

'On all Indian reservations in this country you'll find the people are very discriminatory towards the Indians, and the reason of course is the land. They want their land, and because of this the Indian exists in a kind of pocket where there are prejudicial feelings.'

upon the Indian affirmative over and over again...For through all the slaughter of American Indian biological stocks, the slaughter of their societies and trampling upon their values, strange as it may seem, they have kept their faith. The inner core-value, complex and various, has not been killed.'

He points out how the preserved Indian societies can demonstrate the truth which our age has lost—'that societies are living thing sources of the power and values of the members; that to be and to function in consciously living, aspiring, striving society to be a personality fulfilled, is to be an energ delivered into the communal joy, a partne once more in the cosmic life.

'So the Indian record is the bearer of or great message to the world. Through h

society, and only through his society, man experiences greatness; through it he unites with the universe and the God, and through it, he is freed from all fear. Those who accept the Indian message and lesson will know how intense, even how awful, is the need for creators and creative effort in the field of understanding and discovery of the nature and meaning of the societies of mankind.'

The truth of this rings like a bell through the benighted waters of the Indian oppression. It sounds as a bell of warning to turn the white man from his present course that is bent on destroying a people from whom he, the white man, can learn. This is the one hope that glimmers, however palely, through this chronicle of despair. The white man can learn, he can work towards the peaceful revolution

The preservation of tribal values.

Top left: an infants' school where the children are being taught their own language.

Top right: a girl dressed defiantly in full costume to go to the white man's court.

Bottom: Saturday night dance on the reservation. For once they can relax and be themselves.

that will overthrow the affluent idolatry of his own kind and divert them towards the mystical and creative indivisibility that characterizes the Indians' kinship with their environment. There is optimism to be found in the thinking of the young in America, in the fact that the Love Generation took the values of the tribal society as the substance of their movement. Many went to live with the Hopis in Arizona, to learn from the most withdrawn and peaceful of all the Indian tribes. It was the first collective sign that the white man had given towards the understanding of the Indian manner.

It will not help the Indians if their cause is championed in this way. People who arrive on the reservations, bustling with good intentions, will find themselves faced by the implacable wall of silence which the Indian presents to ideas formed in the white man's mind and couched in the white man's terms. The act of helping the Indians is no good if it only benefits the helpers. A question will be answered with a mono-syllable, nothing given away. Ask them if they are angry and they will look at you as if they do not know the meaning of the words. As often

as not, the question is not important to them, representing only the excitability of the white man. Besides it is interference, however well-meaning, and how can they believe that the white man will understand them now, suddenly, when he has failed to do so for nearly five hundred years? When questions are asked of young Indians, their silence may be rooted in a different reason. If they have come back to the reservations from the boarding school, they find that they ask themselves the question – 'Am I going to answer like an Indian or am I going to answer like the outside culture?' If they can come to terms with this confusion, they can be the pillars of the bridge between the two societies. At present, however, the traffic is one way. The tribal *mores* that come out of the reservations help the young Americans. Only in the long distant and rose-coloured future, when the white man has changed his way, will it help the Indian. In the meantime there has to be hope that by that far-off day the Indians will not have disappeared into the whirlpool, and lost that culture which could be the very renaissance of their continent.

A great deal depends on how much the Indians are prepared to help themselves. Conditions are visibly better on the reservations which have energetic and efficient tribal leaders.

It will take a long time, this apprehension of the Indian mind. The white man will never be fully immersed in it, but he can be adaptive to it. The obstacles to be overcome are enormous, not least among them the workings of the bureaucracy. A story is told of a meeting called by a Bureau worker to discuss grazing rights with the tribal council. The Bureau worker arrives on time, the Indians appear an hour later. That is Indian time; if you call a meeting for six o'clock it will start at seven. The Indians sit down at the meeting, and gaze at their folded hands. The minutes go by and no one speaks. After a long time one of them grunts, and another answers, monosyllabically. There is silence again. Eventually after an hour of contemplation they rise and file out. The BIA man, having sat for two hours in silence, is trying to suppress his rage. He follows the Indians and asks one of them why they refused to speak at the meeting. The Indian replies that the question of the grazing rights is very hard, and that people will be hurt by it. But, he adds that they feel better about it now because it was peaceful sitting there thinking it over. The BIA worker sighs and looks heavenward. 'They call that discussing,' he says.

The white man has to overcome centuries of contempt in order to learn patience with these ways. This applies especially to the system of land leasing on the reservations, which is corrupt by any standards. Through a complicated procedure of inheritance an Indian may own several hundred acres on a reservation but it will be divided into a series of small plots, often miles apart. The sections are generally so small that the owner may not know where they are. In any case few portions are large enough for him to farm. As a result the small units are consolidated by the BIA to form parts of larger units which are then leased by the Bureau to mainly white ranchers. The problem of inheritance, created by the fact that very few Indians left wills, can likewise mean that there are several hundred heirs to a tiny plot of land. The BIA leases out this land also to white ranchers, and the money is divided among the owners. In both these cases, the Indian receives a pittance. Many such land-owning Indians are themselves unemployed, and this creates the unique situation in which the estate owners are the poorest people in the area. The fact that this continues is governed in part by the contempt of the ranchers who graze the land, and do very well by it. When confronted with the ethics of the problem, they will tend to shrug and pass off their responsibility with the aside that a group of lazy Injuns could never be bothered with making anything of the land. To hold such an attitude is to forget that the Indians have never adjusted themselves to the absence of limitless space. The Indian would make good use of the land, if it was there to make use of, but he would do it in the way that suited him, as part of his special relationship with it. The question to him is not one of profitability but of subsistence, of fulfilling his needs.

The white man differs in his understanding of time and of money. One of the reasons why there are so few factories on reservations is the impatience of the businessmen with the Indians' inability to conform to normal working hours. To the Indians, this is a pettiness. Their ideal

Indians in the United States Today

(excluding Alaska)

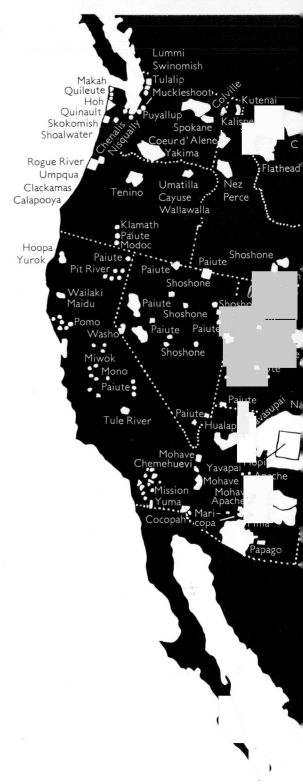

is to come and go from work when they please, operating without a clock, working for twenty-four hours at a stretch perhaps and then taking two days off to fish. They would wish to be paid for what they have done. It suits the Indian style, enabling them to benefit from the white man's world and still retain that independence so integral to their Indianness.

Given the opportunity and the right framework within which to work, they can achieve those things of which white society believes them incapable. It is where they are scorned that they react with a stubborn refusal to compromise, and the white boss congratulates himself on the confirmation of his opinion : 'The people that are educated and knowledge-able leave the reservation, and consequently the type of personnel that is left is very limited. You're really scraping the bottom of the barrel.' He sees the Indians as incompetent, not only in their working habits but in their handling of the money they earn. 'The consensus of opinion is ''There's no tomorrow. Tomorrow will never come so let's have fun today.'' So consequently they might go down and spend their pay cheque on Friday on liquor and wine and have a good weekend. Well, it's two weeks to the next pay cheque, so they are in trouble. They have to beg, borrow

and steal whatever they can get in the interim

The problem of alcoholism is certainly severe and adds fuel to the white man's contempt. H can argue with conviction that any money donated to the tribes will be drunk away. Th Indian today is no better equipped to withstan the effects of drink than he was in the past, an with the stresses of the moment, both on an off the reservations, it is hard to resist th temptation. The Indians who have been re located to the cities and been reduced to Ski Row alcoholics bring their addiction back wit them if they return to the reservation. The continue to drink because they have been awa and failed, and have come back to their ow people who are themselves drinking becaus life on the reservation is so empty and they ca see what it does to those who leave it. Thes two groups are often in conflict, the cit Indians scorning the reservation natives fo their unsophistication, the reservation Indian scorning the city dropouts for being infecte by the white man. But the conflict creates further confusion, leaving all but the mos traditionalist in a limbo, uncertain of what i best for them. The only real self-assurance t be found among the Indians is seen in those wh have either been totally assimilated, ar successful executives etc. (in effect, whit

Previous page: ' They are tied by the invisible bonds to the land . . .'

This page: to be true to their Indianness is now more real than to be true to their tribal traditions. For ceremonial occasions, and for the benefit of the tourists, some wear head-dresses which their ancestors never wore.

Opposite: the urge to remain separate is strong. Even comparatively affluent city workers return to the reservation at the weekends.

men), and in those who remain intractably Indian. The vast majority are in the vacuum in between, travelling by car to the drive-in movie, returning to their unlit hovel.

There is nothing much in reservation life that can keep the unhappy people from the bars. The white man sowed another disease on the wind when he defeated the Indians. Boredom. They had never known it before. It hangs in the reservation air with oppressive stillness, sapping their energies, feeding their despair. It affects particularly the unemployed, and the young, both of whom have nothing to do. While the Navajo shepherd is at peace with his flock, the Navajo adolescent, back from the boarding school, is adrift in his despondency. He has broken his relationship with the earth, and on the reservation there are none of the white man's entertainments to pass the time. The older people, in those areas where it is available, can transcend their difficulties through the timeless ritual of peyote, the non-addictive drug which creates hallucinatory effects and is taken in a ceremony that is closely linked with their religion. Alcohol does not produce that same reflective calm, which is what they need most of all when their Indian-ness has been purloined and they cannot dismiss their boredom.

The most depressing products of alcoholism are to be seen among the returning soldiers. They have returned from the Pacific, from Korea, from Vietnam, where they have acquired reputations for coolness and bravery in battle. For a short time, the white society for whom they have fought remembers them and honours their valour. Then they go back to their reservations, and nothing is different except themselves. They have been engaged in two wars simultaneously—a military war on the battlefield and a cultural war in the barracks. Their people are proud of their bravery but resistant to their contamination. Restless and confused, the soldiers have too many ghosts to exorcise. The bars fill up with war heroes for whom the spectacle of the reservations is scarcely less ruinous than what they have seen at the front. They take as their symbol the hero of the Marine Corps, Ira Hayes, who raised the flag at Iwo Jima. When Hayes returned to the United States he was feted and decorated. When the feasting was over he travelled back to the Pima Reservation in Arizona. An exemplary soldier, he found himself unemployed and forgotten. He became an alcoholic, 'the whiskey-drinking Ira Hayes', and died in a drainage ditch in two inches of water. His death is seen as the ultimate betrayal.

The story of the Indian from 1492 until today is filled with contradictions that can be assessed, but not resolved, dispassionately. The white man will always have his statement for the defence—the disillusionment of many welfare workers among the Indians today strengthens his protestations of innocence, as do his own oft-repeated good intentions, financial statistics of help proffered, and his disclaiming of the behaviour of his ancestors (but which, he will say, can be justified by the greatness of America today). The Indian will always have his simple argument that he was happy before Columbus came and ever since he has had to combat robbery and oppression. In this complex and sophisticated age it is almost ingenuous to

separated from it once and for all; the Indian saw his culture gradually eroding before his very eyes. The Negro, once in the New World, was individualistic rather than tribal; the Indian has always been group-minded. The Negro, even though he was in slavery to the white man and at the lowest end of the human scale, was at the same time appended to the white society. If he was to progress, he could only move upwards. The Indian, being detached, had no such opportunity, and, being detached, never desired it. The adjustments that he has to make now if he does choose the white man's way are greater and more complex than those confronting the Negro. Likewise, because of his detachment, the Indian has suffered vilification of a most pernicious nature.

'. . . . and when the last Red Man shall have perished, and the memory of my tribe shall have become a myth among the White Men, these shores will swarm with the invisible dead of my tribe . . .'

side so literally and completely with the Indian, but if it is possible to step outside the machinations of time itself, as the Indian does, and to search for a single cosmic truth in the chronicle of their history, then it is impossible to turn away from the belief that night entered their future with the arrival of Columbus and that it has not lifted since. If there is light in the sky, it can be seen only in the most optimistic assessments of the nature of mankind, only in the most idealistic prophecy of the world's future.

Comparisons with other suppressed races, either now or in the past, add nothing to the arguments. Many will seek to relate the lot of the Indian today with that of the Negro. The only parallel between the two, in the continent of America, is that both have been persecuted. Their persecution was sometimes related—the treatment of the Indians, in the Southeast particularly, led to the subsequent treatment of the Negroes there. To justify their cruelty to the Five Civilized Tribes, the Georgia whites had to continue in the same vein with the Negroes. In other respects, there is no direct analogy to be drawn. The Negro may have been divorced from his original culture, but when he came to America he was physically

Nothing so enrages a conquering race as their inability to understand the people they conquer, because then they find it compulsive to despise.

The tragedy of the Indian decline revolves around the unalterable character of two contrasting cultures. It is easy to look at this conflict and discuss it with careless aphorisms about East being East and West being West. But that helps not at all and gives comfort to the theory that the only lesson we learn from history is that we learn no lesson from history. Such evasion will not prompt the white man to learn from the Indian way and will only serve to assuage his guilt. The hope must be that the blood has not obliterated reason, and that before it is too late, the whites will absorb some understanding from a world they have all but destroyed.

It is equally escapist to elevate the fall of the Indians to the level of poetic tragedy, deriving a false comfort from the doomed nature of their destiny. Mark Twain suggested that no people could have resisted the temptations of a civilization that offered booze, gunbarrels *and* Bibles. The remark may have been sardonic, but still reflects the popular death wish which the Americans felt for the natives, which they hoped would be realized so that they could mourn their passing with the sincerity that nations reserve for their myths. As a young cadet, George Custer wrote: 'The red man is alone in his misery. We behold him now on the verge of extinction, standing on his last foothold ...and soon he will be talked of as a noble race who once existed but have passed away'. Ten years later Custer committed his barbarity on the Washita River. The motto of the only good Indian being a dead Indian was rooted in more complex emotions than may at first have appeared. They are emotions which persist today, retaining their complexity. In the concealed hope that the Indians may yet be the 'vanishing Americans', their story is recorded on the epic scale, so that their doom may be seen as inescapable. The theory of pre-destination thus assists the white man to evade his responsibility towards them.

White attitudes towards the Indians have always seemed to veer between extremes. In the past, if they were not Noble Red Men then they were contemptible savages. Both views were based in mythology, but sadly it has always been the derogatory one which has dominated the thinking and led to harsh

mentary presented to them which would help divorce them from their myths. It is rare, for instance, to read an account such as George Bird Grinnell's of his stay with the Pawnees in 1888: 'It was the last day of my stay at the Pawnee agency. I had seen many an old friend, had laughed and joked with some over incidents of former years, and with others had mourned over brave warriors or wise old men who were no longer with us. My visit had been full of pleasure, and yet full of pain. When I had first known the tribe (1870) it numbered more than three thousand people, now there are only a little more than eight hundred of them. The evidences of their progress toward civilization are cheering. They are now self-supporting. They no longer die of hunger. But the character of the people has changed. In the old barbaric days they were light-hearted, merry makers of jokes, keenly alive to the humorous side of life. Now they are serious, grave, little disposed to laugh. Then they were like children without a care. Now they are like men, on whom the anxieties of life weigh heavily. Civilization, bringing with it some measure of material prosperity, has also brought to these people care, responsibility, repression. No doubt it is best, and it is inevitable, but it is sad, too.'

policies. Many easterners, for example, in the nineteenth century, were genuinely sympathetic towards 'book' Indians, but this made no appreciable difference to the actual treatment of the natives in the east and certainly did nothing to lessen the harassment of the Indians in the west. Today the viewpoints waver between seeing the Indian as a lazy and backward incompetent to seeing him as the noble survivor of a priceless culture. Again both are unreal images, and again it is the derogatory attitude that controls the official line.

It is unfortunate in this respect that so little is known on a broad scale about the Indian as a person. Few individuals have adopted a positive approach towards the native, and the general public have therefore had little genuine com-

The conclusion may be pious, but the expression of warmth towards the Indians is unique. It is almost without precedent for a white individual to describe his friendship with Indians in the same way that he would describe friendships with his own kind.

Today the reservation Indians, increasingly withdrawn where they seek to avoid the urban sickness, are more difficult to know. They remain suspicious of interference, knowing that the solicitous inquiries of whites are too often the ingenious workings of bureaucracy disguised as humanity. They do not have, and never have had, the habit of small talk. Those that move in the political circles of the white man, working for the welfare of their peoples, find themselves in the round of diplomatic

parties and the Indianness seeps from them in the chatter and intrigue. Assimilation works at the highest level, so the reservation Indians become suspicious of their own kind. They believe perhaps that nothing good will ever come to them in the way of restoring to them their lost rights, and they retire into their private philosophy.

'The Indian believes that he is a cannibal – all of his life he must eat his brothers and his sisters and deer and corn which is the mother, and the fish which is the brother. All our lives we must eat off them and be a cannibal, but when we die then we can give back all that we have taken, and our body goes to feed the worms that feed the birds. And it feeds the roots of the trees and the grass so that the deer can eat it and the birds can nest in the tree. And we can give back. But today we can't even do this, you know. They poison our bodies and

meaning, has purpose. But the more strongly their parents infuse them with its importance, the deeper the confusion of the children when they return from the white man's school. 'I was raised with all the tradition and all the rules and regulations and instructions and I pass these on to the young ones, and now I find that the young ones are coming back from school where they have been told that we are an inferior race, subhuman, that we were savages...' Some of the older Indians believe that the power of their inheritance, and the unarguable strength of their approach to life will be enough to retain their children in their Indianness, and help them to build a peace from their confusion. 'I think we will still win, I think there are enough people who wish to understand the Indian mind, that we are not going to harm anyone, that we are peaceful people, we are not aggressive people. In this lies our strength and

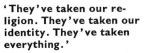

we can't bury our people. We have to be put in boxes to wait for some life, you know, that's going to be...We are all going to rise up, which is so...different from the way we feel about our bodies and giving back.'

It is the ancient, guarded and selfless relationship with nature and the forces of nature. 'We want freedom from the white man rather than to be integrated. We don't want any part of the establishment, we want to be free to raise our children in our religion, in our ways, to be able to hunt and fish and to live in peace. We want to live off the land, to follow the sacred instructions given to us by the Creator when he put us on this land, to live with nature, the divine laws of nature which join the laws of the Creator. We don't want power, we don't want to be congressmen, bankers, we want to be ourselves. We want to have our own religion and to raise our children to be proud of our heritage, because we are the owners of this land and because we belong here.'

The Indians preserve their heritage for their children. For them, as for no other children within America, the whole Indian tradition has

from here we will pick up. I believe that we will survive, I still believe we will survive. That is our dream.'

The Indian harbours his mysticism and hands down his heritage. It has an unreal quality amid the shacks of the reservations. In the bars the bodies roll, insensible with drink. The transistors blare out, and the accidie hangs in the air. At the tourist centres, Indians leap before the white man's cameras, wearing head-dresses their tribes never knew. On the prairies the Sioux revive the Sun Dance. The ancient private half-forgotten tribal patterns weave before the nodding elders. Their chests pierced by skewers, the dancers perform with the dark intensity that will heighten their vision and conquer their pain. The drum-beat bounces from the battered hulks of cars. Thump, thump, thump. 'The white man says there is freedom and justice for all. We have had "freedom and justice", and that is why we have been almost exterminated. These are just words in the wind.'

Index

The Publishers are grateful to the following for permission to reproduce quotations: Pp 12, 97, 100: University of Nebraska Press. John G. Neihardt, *Black Elk Speaks*. P 138: University of Nebraska Press. George Bird Grinnell, *Pawnee Hero Stories and Folk Tales*.
P 32: © Copyright 1953, The University of New Mexico Press. George P. Hammond and Agapito Rey, *Don Juan de Oñate, Colonizer of New Mexico, 1595–1628, Part I*.
P 100: Granada Publishing Limited. William Carlos Williams, *In the American Grain*; New Directions Publishing Corporation. William Carlos Williams, *In the American Grain*.
P 50: © Copyright 1961, American Heritage Publishing Company, Inc. *The American Heritage Book of Indians*.
Pp 125, 126, 127: The New American Library Inc. John Collier, *Indians of the Americas*.
Thames Television for making transcript material available from which direct quotations have been taken.
Illustrations reproduced by courtesy of: American Museum of Natural History 16 and 17; British Museum 23; Bureau of Indian Affairs 121, 125; Chicago Historical Society *37t*, *38 t*; Collection Musee de l'Homme 54 t; Denver Public Library 58 and 59, 138; Mike Fash Associates front jacket, 104, 105, *56, 82 and 83, 84 b, 109, 127*; Nino La Femina *84 r, 128 l*; Freelance Photographers' Guild 85, *38 r, 55*; Thomas Gilcrease Institute *10 and 11, 38 l*; Globe Photos: John R. Hamilton *9*; G. D. Hackett 28, 66, 68 l, 69 l, 88, 89, 92, 96, 97, 100, 101, 111, 115 r, 116, 117, 120, 124, 129, 134, 135, 139; Librairie Larousse 14, 18 and 19, 27 r; Library of Congress 26, 27 l, 61 tr, 74 t, 74 and 75 b, 76 and 77; Magnum Photos: Burk Uzzle 90 and 91, 93, 98 and 99, 102 and 103, 112 and 113, 118 and 119, 122 and 123, 132 and 133, 136, 137; M-G-M 87 b; Minnesota Historical Society 47, 61 l, 63 t, 67, 73 t, 78 t, 78 b, 79 b; Keith Morris *81*; Museum of New Mexico Collection 60 l; Museum of Modern Art, New York 114 and 115; Museum of the American Indian *12*; National Archives 72 t; National Film Archives 86, 87 t; New York Historical Society 32, 33; New York Public Library *37 t*, 52 and 53; Oklahoma Historical Society 62; Peabody Museum, Harvard University 50; Pennsylvania Academy of Fine Arts 24 and 25; Public Archives of Canada 15 b, 22, 42, 43, 44, 45; Royal Ontario Museum 46; Seattle Public Library title page, 140 and 141; Smithsonian Institution, Bureau of American Ethnology Collection back jacket 13 b, 20, 21, 36, 39, 48 and 49, 51, 52 t, 54 b, 61 br, 68 r, 70 and 71, 73 b, 79 t; State Historical Society of Colorado 63 b, 69 r; Thames Television Ltd 94 and 95, 106 and 107, 108 t, 108b, 126; Ron Thomas *110, 128 r, 128 b*; University of Oklahoma Library 75 t; US Signal Corps 13 t, 35, 57, 72 b, 80; Weaver-Smith Collection 15 t, 64 and 65; Yale University Library 34, 40; Z F A 84 c.
Film stills reproduced by courtesy of: Metro-Goldwyn-Mayer Pictures Ltd: 'How the West Was Won'
United Artists Corporation Ltd: 'Comanche'
MCA (England) TV Ltd: 'The Plainsman' (Paramount)